D0426134

THIS JOURNAL
BELONGS TO:

....

....

....

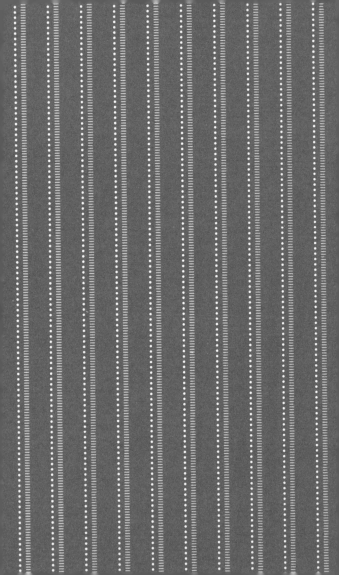

FIVE-YEAR
MEMORY
JOURNAL
• 366 •
Thought-Provoking Prompts
to Create Your Own
Life Chronicle

*"The aim of life is self-development.
To realize one's nature perfectly—
that is what each of us is here for."*
—Oscar Wilde

You can start this keepsake journal on any day of the year.
Just go to today's date, read the prompt and start writing.
There are five entry spaces on every page, for you to enter
your responses each year over the next five years.

STERLING
New York

An Imprint of Sterling Publishing
387 Park Avenue South
New York, NY 10016

ISBN 978-1-4549-1127-2

Distributed in Canada by Sterling Publishing
c/o Canadian Manda Group, 165 Dufferin Street
Toronto, Ontario, Canada M6K 3H6
Distributed in the United Kingdom by GMC Distribution Services
Castle Place, 166 High Street, Lewes, East Sussex, England BN7 1XU
Distributed in Australia by Capricorn Link (Australia) Pty. Ltd.
P.O. Box 704, Windsor, NSW 2756, Australia

For information about custom editions, special sales,
and premium and corporate purchases, please contact
Sterling Special Sales at 800-805-5489
or specialsales@sterlingpublishing.com.

Manufactured in China

6 8 10 9 7

www.sterlingpublishing.com

JANUARY 1

My New Year's resolution this year is . . .

20___ ___ * _____

_____

_____

20___ ___ * _____

_____

_____

20___ ___ * _____

_____

_____

20___ ___ * _____

_____

_____

20___ ___ * _____

_____

_____

JANUARY 2

The first song I heard today was . . .

20 __ __ * _____

_____

_____

20 __ __ * _____

_____

_____

20 __ __ * _____

_____

_____

20 __ __ * _____

_____

_____

20 __ __ * _____

_____

_____

JANUARY 3

I wish . . . could have been with me when I . . .

20___ ___ * _____

_____

_____

20___ ___ * _____

_____

_____

20___ ___ * _____

_____

_____

20___ ___ * _____

_____

_____

20___ ___ * _____

_____

_____

JANUARY 4

Money isn't an option. The first thing I would buy is . . .

20___ ___ * _____

_____

_____

_____

20___ ___ * _____

_____

_____

_____

20___ ___ * _____

_____

_____

_____

20___ ___ * _____

_____

_____

_____

20___ ___ * _____

_____

_____

_____

JANUARY 5

If I had one phone call left, I would call . . .

20___ ___ * _____

_____

_____

_____

20___ ___ * _____

_____

_____

_____

20___ ___ * _____

_____

_____

_____

20___ ___ * _____

_____

_____

_____

20___ ___ * _____

_____

_____

_____

JANUARY 6

My secret fantasy is . . .

20___ ___ * _____
_____
_____
|||||||||||||||||||||||||||||||||||||||||||||||||||||||||||||||||||||||||||||||||||||||||||||||||||||||||||||||||||||||||||||

20___ ___ * _____
_____
_____
|||||||||||||||||||||||||||||||||||||||||||||||||||||||||||||||||||||||||||||||||||||||||||||||||||||||||||||||||||||||||||||

20___ ___ * _____
_____
_____
|||||||||||||||||||||||||||||||||||||||||||||||||||||||||||||||||||||||||||||||||||||||||||||||||||||||||||||||||||||||||||||

20___ ___ * _____
_____
_____
|||||||||||||||||||||||||||||||||||||||||||||||||||||||||||||||||||||||||||||||||||||||||||||||||||||||||||||||||||||||||||||

20___ ___ * _____
_____
_____
|||||||||||||||||||||||||||||||||||||||||||||||||||||||||||||||||||||||||||||||||||||||||||||||||||||||||||||||||||||||||||||

I wish I could tell the entire world . . .

20 __ __ * _____

_____

_____

_____

20 __ __ * _____

_____

_____

_____

20 __ __ * _____

_____

_____

_____

20 __ __ * _____

_____

_____

_____

20 __ __ * _____

_____

_____

_____

JANUARY 8

I need . . . to face my biggest fear of the moment.

20___ ___ * _____

_____

_____

20___ ___ * _____

_____

_____

20___ ___ * _____

_____

_____

20___ ___ * _____

_____

_____

20___ ___ * _____

_____

_____

JANUARY 9

My celebrity crush is . . .

20 __ __ * _____

_____

_____

20 __ __ * _____

_____

_____

20 __ __ * _____

_____

_____

20 __ __ * _____

_____

_____

20 __ __ * _____

_____

_____

JANUARY 10

I remember . . . from my childhood

20___ ___ * _____
_____
_____
_____

20___ ___ * _____
_____
_____
_____

20___ ___ * _____
_____
_____
_____

20___ ___ * _____
_____
_____
_____

20___ ___ * _____
_____
_____
_____

JANUARY 11

My relationship status is . . .

20___ ___ * _____

_____

_____

20___ ___ * _____

_____

_____

20___ ___ * _____

_____

_____

20___ ___ * _____

_____

_____

20___ ___ * _____

_____

_____

JANUARY 12

My biggest flaw is . . .

20___ ___ * _____

_____

_____

_____

20___ ___ * _____

_____

_____

_____

20___ ___ * _____

_____

_____

_____

20___ ___ * _____

_____

_____

_____

20___ ___ * _____

_____

_____

_____

JANUARY 13

A compliment I received today was . . .

20___ ___ * _____

_____

_____

20___ ___ * _____

_____

_____

20___ ___ * _____

_____

_____

20___ ___ * _____

_____

_____

20___ ___ * _____

_____

_____

JANUARY 14

I would most like to learn the . . . language.

20___ ___ * _____

_____

_____

_____

20___ ___ * _____

_____

_____

_____

20___ ___ * _____

_____

_____

_____

20___ ___ * _____

_____

_____

_____

20___ ___ * _____

_____

_____

_____

JANUARY 15

I feel . . . years old today.

20___ ___ * _____

_____

_____

_____

20___ ___ * _____

_____

_____

_____

20___ ___ * _____

_____

_____

_____

20___ ___ * _____

_____

_____

_____

20___ ___ * _____

_____

_____

_____

Today, the most interesting question
someone asked me was . . .

20___ ___ * _____

_____

_____

|||||||||||||||||||||||||||||||||||||||||||||||||||||||||||||||||||||||||||||||||

20___ ___ * _____

_____

_____

|||||||||||||||||||||||||||||||||||||||||||||||||||||||||||||||||||||||||||||||||

20___ ___ * _____

_____

_____

|||||||||||||||||||||||||||||||||||||||||||||||||||||||||||||||||||||||||||||||||

20___ ___ * _____

_____

_____

|||||||||||||||||||||||||||||||||||||||||||||||||||||||||||||||||||||||||||||||||

20___ ___ * _____

_____

_____

|||||||||||||||||||||||||||||||||||||||||||||||||||||||||||||||||||||||||||||||||

JANUARY 17

Today I tried . . .

20 __ __ * _____

_____

_____

_____

20 __ __ * _____

_____

_____

_____

20 __ __ * _____

_____

_____

_____

20 __ __ * _____

_____

_____

_____

20 __ __ * _____

_____

_____

_____

JANUARY 18

. . . is on my mind right now.

20__ __ * _____
_____
_____
_____

20__ __ * _____
_____
_____
_____

20__ __ * _____
_____
_____
_____

20__ __ * _____
_____
_____
_____

20__ __ * _____
_____
_____
_____

JANUARY 19

The animal I wish to be is . . .

20__ __ * _____

_____

_____

20__ __ * _____

_____

_____

20__ __ * _____

_____

_____

20__ __ * _____

_____

_____

20__ __ * _____

_____

_____

JANUARY 20

Tomorrow, I am looking forward to . . .

20__ __ * _____

_____

_____

20__ __ * _____

_____

_____

20__ __ * _____

_____

_____

20__ __ * _____

_____

_____

20__ __ * _____

_____

_____

JANUARY 21

People say I look like . . .

20___ ___ ＊ _____

_____

_____

20___ ___ ＊ _____

_____

_____

20___ ___ ＊ _____

_____

_____

20___ ___ ＊ _____

_____

_____

20___ ___ ＊ _____

_____

_____

JANUARY 22

Today is special because . . .

20___ ___ * _____
_____
_____
||||||||||||||||||||||||||||||||||||||||||||||||||||||||||||||||||||||||||||||||||||||||||||||||||||||||||||||||||||||||||||

20___ ___ * _____
_____
_____
||||||||||||||||||||||||||||||||||||||||||||||||||||||||||||||||||||||||||||||||||||||||||||||||||||||||||||||||||||||||||||

20___ ___ * _____
_____
_____
||||||||||||||||||||||||||||||||||||||||||||||||||||||||||||||||||||||||||||||||||||||||||||||||||||||||||||||||||||||||||||

20___ ___ * _____
_____
_____
||||||||||||||||||||||||||||||||||||||||||||||||||||||||||||||||||||||||||||||||||||||||||||||||||||||||||||||||||||||||||||

20___ ___ * _____
_____
_____
||||||||||||||||||||||||||||||||||||||||||||||||||||||||||||||||||||||||||||||||||||||||||||||||||||||||||||||||||||||||||||

JANUARY 23

Right now I am . . .

20__ __ * _____

_____

_____

_____

20__ __ * _____

_____

_____

_____

20__ __ * _____

_____

_____

_____

20__ __ * _____

_____

_____

_____

20__ __ * _____

_____

_____

_____

JANUARY 24

I am planning . . .

20__ __ * _____
_____
_____
_____

20__ __ * _____
_____
_____
_____

20__ __ * _____
_____
_____
_____

20__ __ * _____
_____
_____
_____

20__ __ * _____
_____
_____
_____

JANUARY 25

I am nervous about . . .

20___ ___ * _____

_____

_____

20___ ___ * _____

_____

_____

20___ ___ * _____

_____

_____

20___ ___ * _____

_____

_____

20___ ___ * _____

_____

_____

JANUARY 26

Today I paid it forward by . . .

20___ ___ ＊ _____

_____

_____

20___ ___ ＊ _____

_____

_____

20___ ___ ＊ _____

_____

_____

20___ ___ ＊ _____

_____

_____

20___ ___ ＊ _____

_____

_____

JANUARY 27

The last thing I did for the "first time" was . . .

20__ __ * _____

_____

_____

20__ __ * _____

_____

_____

20__ __ * _____

_____

_____

20__ __ * _____

_____

_____

20__ __ * _____

_____

_____

JANUARY 28

Advice I would give to myself at this time a year ago is . . .

20___ ___ * _____

_____

_____

_____

20___ ___ * _____

_____

_____

_____

20___ ___ * _____

_____

_____

_____

20___ ___ * _____

_____

_____

_____

20___ ___ * _____

_____

_____

_____

JANUARY 29

Today I was encouraged by . . .

20___ ___ * _____

_____

_____

_____

20___ ___ * _____

_____

_____

_____

20___ ___ * _____

_____

_____

_____

20___ ___ * _____

_____

_____

_____

20___ ___ * _____

_____

_____

_____

JANUARY 30

The song I hate to love is . . .

20___ ___ * _____

_____

_____

20___ ___ * _____

_____

_____

20___ ___ * _____

_____

_____

20___ ___ * _____

_____

_____

20___ ___ * _____

_____

_____

JANUARY 31

. . . is my favorite relative because . . .

20___ ___ * _____

_____

_____

20___ ___ * _____

_____

_____

20___ ___ * _____

_____

_____

20___ ___ * _____

_____

_____

20___ ___ * _____

_____

_____

_____

FEBRUARY 1

If I could be two places at once, today I would go . . .

20___ ___ * _____

_____

_____

_____

20___ ___ * _____

_____

_____

_____

20___ ___ * _____

_____

_____

_____

20___ ___ * _____

_____

_____

_____

20___ ___ * _____

_____

_____

_____

FEBRUARY 2

The last "best" meal I cooked was . . .

20___ ___ * _____

_____

_____

20___ ___ * _____

_____

_____

20___ ___ * _____

_____

_____

20___ ___ * _____

_____

_____

20___ ___ * _____

_____

_____

FEBRUARY 3

The last tough decision I made was . . .

20___ ___ * _____
_____
_____
_____

20___ ___ * _____
_____
_____
_____

20___ ___ * _____
_____
_____
_____

20___ ___ * _____
_____
_____
_____

20___ ___ * _____
_____
_____
_____

FEBRUARY 4

Right now I have a yen for . . .

20 __ __ * _____

_____

_____

20 __ __ * _____

_____

_____

20 __ __ * _____

_____

_____

20 __ __ * _____

_____

_____

20 __ __ * _____

_____

_____

FEBRUARY 5

The last news headline that made me happy was . . .

20___ ___ * _____

_____

_____

_____

20___ ___ * _____

_____

_____

_____

20___ ___ * _____

_____

_____

_____

20___ ___ * _____

_____

_____

_____

20___ ___ * _____

_____

_____

_____

FEBRUARY 6

The longest I went without using technology today is . . .

20 __ __ * _____

_____

_____

20 __ __ * _____

_____

_____

20 __ __ * _____

_____

_____

20 __ __ * _____

_____

_____

20 __ __ * _____

_____

_____

FEBRUARY 7

The last time I "fell in love" with something/someone was . . .

20___ ___ * _____

_____

_____

20___ ___ * _____

_____

_____

20___ ___ * _____

_____

_____

20___ ___ * _____

_____

_____

20___ ___ * _____

_____

_____

FEBRUARY 8

If I have a crisis, the first person I call is . . .

20___ ___ * _____

_____

_____

20___ ___ * _____

_____

_____

20___ ___ * _____

_____

_____

20___ ___ * _____

_____

_____

20___ ___ * _____

_____

_____

One moment I wish to relive from the past year is . . .

20___ ___ * _____

_____

_____

20___ ___ * _____

_____

_____

20___ ___ * _____

_____

_____

20___ ___ * _____

_____

_____

20___ ___ * _____

_____

_____

FEBRUARY 10

My personal slogan would be . . .

20___ ___ * _____

_____

_____

_____

20___ ___ * _____

_____

_____

_____

20___ ___ * _____

_____

_____

_____

20___ ___ * _____

_____

_____

_____

20___ ___ * _____

_____

_____

_____

FEBRUARY 11

Describe the strangest recent dream you remember.

20 __ __ * _____

_____

_____

20 __ __ * _____

_____

_____

20 __ __ * _____

_____

_____

20 __ __ * _____

_____

_____

20 __ __ * _____

_____

_____

FEBRUARY 12

Describe your best friend in one word.

20___ ___ * _____

_____

_____

20___ ___ * _____

_____

_____

20___ ___ * _____

_____

_____

20___ ___ * _____

_____

_____

20___ ___ * _____

_____

_____

FEBRUARY 13

The one thing I need help with is . . .

20___ ___ * _____

_____

_____

_____

20___ ___ * _____

_____

_____

_____

20___ ___ * _____

_____

_____

_____

20___ ___ * _____

_____

_____

_____

20___ ___ * _____

_____

_____

_____

FEBRUARY 14

If I could spend the next 24 hours
straight with someone, it would be . . .

20___ ___ * _____

_____

_____

20___ ___ * _____

_____

_____

20___ ___ * _____

_____

_____

20___ ___ * _____

_____

_____

20___ ___ * _____

_____

_____

FEBRUARY 15

My last midnight snack was . . .

20__ __ * _____
_____
_____
_____

20__ __ * _____
_____
_____
_____

20__ __ * _____
_____
_____
_____

20__ __ * _____
_____
_____
_____

20__ __ * _____
_____
_____
_____

FEBRUARY 16

I'm afraid to ask . . . this question . . .

20___ ___ * _____

_____

_____

‖‖

20___ ___ * _____

_____

_____

‖‖

20___ ___ * _____

_____

_____

‖‖

20___ ___ * _____

_____

_____

‖‖

20___ ___ * _____

_____

_____

‖‖

FEBRUARY 17

The biggest mistake I made and learned from this year is . . .

20 __ __ * _____

_____

_____

_____

20 __ __ * _____

_____

_____

_____

20 __ __ * _____

_____

_____

_____

20 __ __ * _____

_____

_____

_____

20 __ __ * _____

_____

_____

_____

FEBRUARY 18

Today I am responsible for . . .

20 __ __ * _____

_____

_____

20 __ __ * _____

_____

_____

20 __ __ * _____

_____

_____

20 __ __ * _____

_____

_____

20 __ __ * _____

_____

_____

FEBRUARY 19

I've recently learned how to . . .

20 __ __ ＊ _____

_____

_____

_____

20 __ __ ＊ _____

_____

_____

_____

20 __ __ ＊ _____

_____

_____

_____

20 __ __ ＊ _____

_____

_____

_____

20 __ __ ＊ _____

_____

_____

_____

FEBRUARY 20

If I could give myself an award today, it would be . . .

20___ ___ ✳ _____

_____

_____

20___ ___ ✳ _____

_____

_____

20___ ___ ✳ _____

_____

_____

20___ ___ ✳ _____

_____

_____

20___ ___ ✳ _____

_____

_____

FEBRUARY 21

My go-to de-stresser is . . .

20__ __ * _____

_____

_____

||||||||||||||||||||||||||||||||||||||||||||||||||||||||||||||||||||||||||||||||||||

20__ __ * _____

_____

_____

||||||||||||||||||||||||||||||||||||||||||||||||||||||||||||||||||||||||||||||||||||

20__ __ * _____

_____

_____

||||||||||||||||||||||||||||||||||||||||||||||||||||||||||||||||||||||||||||||||||||

20__ __ * _____

_____

_____

||||||||||||||||||||||||||||||||||||||||||||||||||||||||||||||||||||||||||||||||||||

20__ __ * _____

_____

_____

||||||||||||||||||||||||||||||||||||||||||||||||||||||||||||||||||||||||||||||||||||

FEBRUARY 22

The one world issue I wish I could fix is . . .

20 __ __ * _____

_____

_____

_____

20 __ __ * _____

_____

_____

_____

20 __ __ * _____

_____

_____

_____

20 __ __ * _____

_____

_____

_____

20 __ __ * _____

_____

_____

_____

FEBRUARY 23

One thing I hoped to accomplish this year, but didn't . . .

20___ ___ * _____

_____

_____

20___ ___ * _____

_____

_____

20___ ___ * _____

_____

_____

20___ ___ * _____

_____

_____

20___ ___ * _____

_____

_____

FEBRUARY 24

An idea for an invention I have is . . .

20___ ___ * _____

_____

_____

20___ ___ * _____

_____

_____

20___ ___ * _____

_____

_____

20___ ___ * _____

_____

_____

_____

20___ ___ * _____

_____

_____

FEBRUARY 25

My favorite song to dance to is . . .

20___ ___ * _____

_____

_____

20___ ___ * _____

_____

_____

20___ ___ * _____

_____

_____

20___ ___ * _____

_____

_____

20___ ___ * _____

_____

_____

FEBRUARY 26

The first thing I did when I woke up this morning is . . .

20___ ___ * _____

_____

_____

_____

20___ ___ * _____

_____

_____

_____

20___ ___ * _____

_____

_____

_____

20___ ___ * _____

_____

_____

_____

20___ ___ * _____

_____

_____

_____

FEBRUARY 27

Five things I bought when I last
went grocery shopping are . . .

20___ ___ * _____

_____

_____

_____

20___ ___ * _____

_____

_____

_____

20___ ___ * _____

_____

_____

_____

20___ ___ * _____

_____

_____

_____

20___ ___ * _____

_____

_____

_____

FEBRUARY 28

The strangest thing I heard today was . . .

20__ __ * _____

_____

_____

20__ __ * _____

_____

_____

20__ __ * _____

_____

_____

20__ __ * _____

_____

_____

20__ __ * _____

_____

_____

FEBRUARY 29 (LEAP YEAR)

Today I would like to celebrate me because . . .

20 __ __ * _____

_____

_____

_____

_____

_____

_____

_____

_____

_____

_____

_____

_____

_____

_____

_____

_____

_____

_____

_____

MARCH 1

Something that made me change my mind recently is . . .

20___ ___ * _____

_____

_____

_____

20___ ___ * _____

_____

_____

_____

20___ ___ * _____

_____

_____

_____

20___ ___ * _____

_____

_____

_____

20___ ___ * _____

_____

_____

_____

MARCH 2

The last thing I did that I know I shouldn't have is . . .

20___ ___ * _____

_____

_____

20___ ___ * _____

_____

_____

20___ ___ * _____

_____

_____

20___ ___ * _____

_____

_____

20___ ___ * _____

_____

_____

MARCH 3

A new skill I wish to acquire is . . .

20___ ___ * _____

_____

_____

20___ ___ * _____

_____

_____

20___ ___ * _____

_____

_____

20___ ___ * _____

_____

_____

20___ ___ * _____

_____

_____

MARCH 4

A character from movies or fiction
I wish I could be friends with is . . .

20 ___ ___ ✳ _____

_____

_____

_____

20 ___ ___ ✳ _____

_____

_____

_____

20 ___ ___ ✳ _____

_____

_____

_____

20 ___ ___ ✳ _____

_____

_____

_____

20 ___ ___ ✳ _____

_____

_____

_____

MARCH 5

If I could repaint my walls today, I would paint them . . .

20 __ __ * _____

_____

_____

20 __ __ * _____

_____

_____

20 __ __ * _____

_____

_____

20 __ __ * _____

_____

_____

20 __ __ * _____

_____

_____

MARCH 6

If I could live somewhere else for a year, I would live . . .

20__ __ * _____

_____

_____

20__ __ * _____

_____

_____

20__ __ * _____

_____

_____

20__ __ * _____

_____

_____

20__ __ * _____

_____

_____

MARCH 7

The newest person I've met is . . .

20 __ __ * _____

_____

_____

20 __ __ * _____

_____

_____

20 __ __ * _____

_____

_____

20 __ __ * _____

_____

_____

20 __ __ * _____

_____

_____

Today, I'm most excited for . . .

20___ ___ * _____

_____

_____

20___ ___ * _____

_____

_____

20___ ___ * _____

_____

_____

20___ ___ * _____

_____

_____

20___ ___ * _____

_____

_____

MARCH 9

If it wasn't for . . . , I wouldn't have . . . today.

20___ ___ * _____

_____

_____

_____

20___ ___ * _____

_____

_____

_____

20___ ___ * _____

_____

_____

_____

20___ ___ * _____

_____

_____

_____

20___ ___ * _____

_____

_____

_____

MARCH 10

The newest member of my family is . . .

20___ ___ * _____

_____

_____

‖‖

20___ ___ * _____

_____

_____

‖‖

20___ ___ * _____

_____

_____

‖‖

20___ ___ * _____

_____

_____

‖‖

20___ ___ * _____

_____

_____

‖‖

MARCH 11

The one book I wish I wrote is . . .

20___ ___ * _____

_____

_____

_____

20___ ___ * _____

_____

_____

_____

20___ ___ * _____

_____

_____

_____

20___ ___ * _____

_____

_____

_____

20___ ___ * _____

_____

_____

_____

MARCH 12

One restaurant I keep wanting to try is . . .

20___ ___ * _____
_____
_____

20___ ___ * _____
_____
_____

20___ ___ * _____
_____
_____

20___ ___ * _____
_____
_____

20___ ___ * _____
_____
_____

The perfect amount of money to have
in the bank would be . . . because . . .

20 __ __ * _____

_____

_____

20 __ __ * _____

_____

_____

20 __ __ * _____

_____

_____

20 __ __ * _____

_____

_____

20 __ __ * _____

_____

_____

MARCH 14

*The one thing that's changed about myself
that I wish I could change back is . . .*

20___ ___ * _____

_____

_____

20___ ___ * _____

_____

_____

20___ ___ * _____

_____

_____

20___ ___ * _____

_____

_____

20___ ___ * _____

_____

_____

MARCH 15

One change I would like to see in a year from now is . . .

20___ ___ * _____

_____

_____

20___ ___ * _____

_____

_____

20___ ___ * _____

_____

_____

20___ ___ * _____

_____

_____

20___ ___ * _____

_____

_____

MARCH 16

One thing I am unwilling to negotiate is . . .

20___ ___ * _____

_____

_____

20___ ___ * _____

_____

_____

20___ ___ * _____

_____

_____

20___ ___ * _____

_____

_____

20___ ___ * _____

_____

_____

MARCH 17

One fashion trend I dislike now is . . . , but I love . . .

20___ ___ * _____

_____

_____

20___ ___ * _____

_____

_____

20___ ___ * _____

_____

_____

20___ ___ * _____

_____

_____

20___ ___ * _____

_____

_____

MARCH 18

One thing everyone seems to be talking about lately is . . .

20___ ___ * _____

_____

_____

||||||||||||||||||||||||||||||||||||||||||||||||||||||||||||||||||||||||||||||||||||||||||||||||||||

20___ ___ * _____

_____

_____

||||||||||||||||||||||||||||||||||||||||||||||||||||||||||||||||||||||||||||||||||||||||||||||||||||

20___ ___ * _____

_____

_____

||||||||||||||||||||||||||||||||||||||||||||||||||||||||||||||||||||||||||||||||||||||||||||||||||||

20___ ___ * _____

_____

_____

||||||||||||||||||||||||||||||||||||||||||||||||||||||||||||||||||||||||||||||||||||||||||||||||||||

20___ ___ * _____

_____

_____

||||||||||||||||||||||||||||||||||||||||||||||||||||||||||||||||||||||||||||||||||||||||||||||||||||

MARCH 19

I feel most lonely when . . .

20___ ___ * _____

_____

_____

20___ ___ * _____

_____

_____

20___ ___ * _____

_____

_____

20___ ___ * _____

_____

_____

20___ ___ * _____

_____

_____

MARCH 20

Lyrics that describe my life at the moment are . . .

20__ __ * _____

_____

_____

|||||||||||||||||||||||||||||||||||||||||||||||||||||||||||||||||||||||||||||||||||||||||||||||||

20__ __ * _____

_____

_____

|||||||||||||||||||||||||||||||||||||||||||||||||||||||||||||||||||||||||||||||||||||||||||||||||

20__ __ * _____

_____

_____

|||||||||||||||||||||||||||||||||||||||||||||||||||||||||||||||||||||||||||||||||||||||||||||||||

20__ __ * _____

_____

_____

|||||||||||||||||||||||||||||||||||||||||||||||||||||||||||||||||||||||||||||||||||||||||||||||||

20__ __ * _____

_____

_____

|||||||||||||||||||||||||||||||||||||||||||||||||||||||||||||||||||||||||||||||||||||||||||||||||

MARCH 21

Three words to describe the past year . . .

20___ ___ ＊ _____

_____

_____

_____

20___ ___ ＊ _____

_____

_____

_____

20___ ___ ＊ _____

_____

_____

_____

20___ ___ ＊ _____

_____

_____

_____

20___ ___ ＊ _____

_____

_____

_____

MARCH 22

My most comfortable article of clothing lately is . . .

20___ ___ * _____

_____

_____

20___ ___ * _____

_____

_____

20___ ___ * _____

_____

_____

20___ ___ * _____

_____

_____

20___ ___ * _____

_____

_____

Something I really want to purchase at the moment is . . .

20___ ___ * _____

_____

_____

20___ ___ * _____

_____

_____

20___ ___ * _____

_____

_____

20___ ___ * _____

_____

_____

20___ ___ * _____

_____

_____

MARCH 24

One animal I wish I could have as a pet is . . .

20__ __ * _____

_____

_____

20__ __ * _____

_____

_____

20__ __ * _____

_____

_____

20__ __ * _____

_____

_____

20__ __ * _____

_____

_____

MARCH 25

The last thing that made me really mad was . . .

20 __ __ * _____

_____

_____

20 __ __ * _____

_____

_____

20 __ __ * _____

_____

_____

20 __ __ * _____

_____

_____

20 __ __ * _____

_____

_____

MARCH 26

My favorite quality about my best friend is . . .

20__ __ * _____

_____

_____

20__ __ * _____

_____

_____

20__ __ * _____

_____

_____

20__ __ * _____

_____

_____

20__ __ * _____

_____

_____

MARCH 27

I wish I could spend more time . . .

20___ ___ * _____

_____

_____

_____

20___ ___ * _____

_____

_____

_____

20___ ___ * _____

_____

_____

_____

20___ ___ * _____

_____

_____

_____

20___ ___ * _____

_____

_____

_____

MARCH 28

*One thing about me that I don't
think anyone understands is . . .*

20___ ___ * _____

_____

_____

20___ ___ * _____

_____

_____

20___ ___ * _____

_____

_____

20___ ___ * _____

_____

_____

20___ ___ * _____

_____

_____

One thing I will always remember about
a loved one who has passed away is . . .

20___ ___ * _____

_____

_____

20___ ___ * _____

_____

_____

20___ ___ * _____

_____

_____

20___ ___ * _____

_____

_____

20___ ___ * _____

_____

_____

MARCH 30

A bad habit I recently gave up was . . .

20___ ___ * _____
_____
_____

20___ ___ * _____
_____
_____

20___ ___ * _____
_____
_____

20___ ___ * _____
_____
_____

20___ ___ * _____
_____
_____

MARCH 31

A habit of mine that I cannot shake is . . .

20___ ___ * _____

_____

_____

20___ ___ * _____

_____

_____

20___ ___ * _____

_____

_____

20___ ___ * _____

_____

_____

20___ ___ * _____

_____

_____

APRIL 1

One thing I let others believe
about myself that isn't true is . . .

20_____ * _____

_____

_____

_____

20_____ * _____

_____

_____

_____

20_____ * _____

_____

_____

_____

20_____ * _____

_____

_____

_____

20_____ * _____

_____

_____

_____

APRIL 2

I've learned the most from . . .

20__ __ * _____

_____

_____

20__ __ * _____

_____

_____

20__ __ * _____

_____

_____

20__ __ * _____

_____

_____

20__ __ * _____

_____

_____

APRIL 3

My dream date night would be to . . .

20__ __ ＊ _____

_____

_____

_____

20__ __ ＊ _____

_____

_____

_____

20__ __ ＊ _____

_____

_____

_____

20__ __ ＊ _____

_____

_____

_____

20__ __ ＊ _____

_____

_____

_____

APRIL 4

One meal I wouldn't mind eating everyday
for the rest of my life is . . .

20___ ___ * _____

_____

_____

20___ ___ * _____

_____

_____

20___ ___ * _____

_____

_____

20___ ___ * _____

_____

_____

20___ ___ * _____

_____

_____

APRIL 5

I feel most spiritual when . . .

20___ ___ * _____

_____

_____

20___ ___ * _____

_____

_____

20___ ___ * _____

_____

_____

20___ ___ * _____

_____

_____

20___ ___ * _____

_____

_____

APRIL 6

The last time I had an expectation
that was met was when . . .

20 __ __ * _____

_____

_____

_____

20 __ __ * _____

_____

_____

_____

20 __ __ * _____

_____

_____

_____

20 __ __ * _____

_____

_____

_____

20 __ __ * _____

_____

_____

_____

APRIL 7

Today, I found . . . beautiful because . . .

20___ ___ * _____

_____

_____

_____

20___ ___ * _____

_____

_____

_____

20___ ___ * _____

_____

_____

_____

20___ ___ * _____

_____

_____

_____

20___ ___ * _____

_____

_____

_____

APRIL 8

Something I believe in that others don't is . . .

20___ ___ ✳ _____

_____

_____

20___ ___ ✳ _____

_____

_____

20___ ___ ✳ _____

_____

_____

20___ ___ ✳ _____

_____

_____

20___ ___ ✳ _____

_____

_____

The season that best describes my mood now is . . .

20___ ___ * _____

_____

_____

||||||||||||||||||||||||||||||||||||||||||||||||||||||||||||||||||||||||||||||||||||||||||||

20___ ___ * _____

_____

_____

||||||||||||||||||||||||||||||||||||||||||||||||||||||||||||||||||||||||||||||||||||||||||||

20___ ___ * _____

_____

_____

||||||||||||||||||||||||||||||||||||||||||||||||||||||||||||||||||||||||||||||||||||||||||||

20___ ___ * _____

_____

_____

||||||||||||||||||||||||||||||||||||||||||||||||||||||||||||||||||||||||||||||||||||||||||||

20___ ___ * _____

_____

_____

||||||||||||||||||||||||||||||||||||||||||||||||||||||||||||||||||||||||||||||||||||||||||||

APRIL 10

Children today will never experience . . . like I did.

20___ ___ * _____

_____

_____

_____

20___ ___ * _____

_____

_____

_____

20___ ___ * _____

_____

_____

_____

20___ ___ * _____

_____

_____

_____

20___ ___ * _____

_____

_____

_____

APRIL 11

If I was marooned on a desert island I would need . . .

20__ __ * _____
_____
_____

20__ __ * _____
_____
_____

20__ __ * _____
_____
_____

20__ __ * _____
_____
_____

20__ __ * _____
_____
_____

APRIL 12

My guilty pleasure is . . .

20___ ___ * _____

_____

_____

20___ ___ * _____

_____

_____

20___ ___ * _____

_____

_____

20___ ___ * _____

_____

_____

20___ ___ * _____

_____

_____

APRIL 13

The top three people from history I would
invite to a dinner party are . . .

20__ __ * _____

20__ __ * _____

20__ __ * _____

20__ __ * _____

20__ __ * _____

The first thing I would do if I won the lottery is . . .

20 __ __ * _____

_____

_____

_____

20 __ __ * _____

_____

_____

_____

20 __ __ * _____

_____

_____

_____

20 __ __ * _____

_____

_____

_____

20 __ __ * _____

_____

_____

_____

APRIL 15

If I was a fly on the wall I would want to . . .

20 __ __ ✳ _____

_____

_____

20 __ __ ✳ _____

_____

_____

20 __ __ ✳ _____

_____

_____

20 __ __ ✳ _____

_____

_____

20 __ __ ✳ _____

_____

_____

APRIL 16

People tell me my best feature is . . .

20__ __ * _____

_____

_____

20__ __ * _____

_____

_____

20__ __ * _____

_____

_____

20__ __ * _____

_____

_____

20__ __ * _____

_____

_____

APRIL 17

The very last words I read (before these) were . . .

20___ ___ * _____

_____

_____

20___ ___ * _____

_____

_____

20___ ___ * _____

_____

_____

20___ ___ * _____

_____

_____

20___ ___ * _____

_____

_____

APRIL 18

My current favorite movie is . . . because . . .

20 __ __ * _____

_____

_____

20 __ __ * _____

_____

_____

20 __ __ * _____

_____

_____

20 __ __ * _____

_____

_____

20 __ __ * _____

_____

_____

APRIL 19

I am most proud of . . .

20__ __ * _____

_____

_____

20__ __ * _____

_____

_____

20__ __ * _____

_____

_____

20__ __ * _____

_____

_____

20__ __ * _____

_____

_____

APRIL 20

If I lived a past life, I was probably a . . .

20___ ___ * _____

_____

_____

_____

20___ ___ * _____

_____

_____

_____

20___ ___ * _____

_____

_____

_____

20___ ___ * _____

_____

_____

_____

20___ ___ * _____

_____

_____

_____

APRIL 21

I felt brave when I recently . . .

20___ ___ * _____

_____

_____

20___ ___ * _____

_____

_____

20___ ___ * _____

_____

_____

20___ ___ * _____

_____

_____

20___ ___ * _____

_____

_____

If I could time travel, I would go back to the time of . . .

20___ ___ * _____

_____

_____

20___ ___ * _____

_____

_____

20___ ___ * _____

_____

_____

20___ ___ * _____

_____

_____

20___ ___ * _____

_____

_____

APRIL 23

I look up to . . . as a role model.

20 __ __ * _____

_____

_____

_____

20 __ __ * _____

_____

_____

_____

20 __ __ * _____

_____

_____

_____

20 __ __ * _____

_____

_____

_____

20 __ __ * _____

_____

_____

_____

APRIL 24

The view out my window (or of my surroundings) right now is of . . .

20___ ___ * _____

_____

_____

20___ ___ * _____

_____

_____

20___ ___ * _____

_____

_____

20___ ___ * _____

_____

_____

20___ ___ * _____

_____

_____

APRIL 25

The nicest gift I received recently was . . . , from . . .

20＿＿ * ＿＿＿＿＿＿＿＿＿＿＿＿＿＿＿＿＿＿

＿＿＿＿＿＿＿＿＿＿＿＿＿＿＿＿＿＿＿＿＿＿＿

＿＿＿＿＿＿＿＿＿＿＿＿＿＿＿＿＿＿＿＿＿＿＿

20＿＿ * ＿＿＿＿＿＿＿＿＿＿＿＿＿＿＿＿＿＿

＿＿＿＿＿＿＿＿＿＿＿＿＿＿＿＿＿＿＿＿＿＿＿

＿＿＿＿＿＿＿＿＿＿＿＿＿＿＿＿＿＿＿＿＿＿＿

20＿＿ * ＿＿＿＿＿＿＿＿＿＿＿＿＿＿＿＿＿＿

＿＿＿＿＿＿＿＿＿＿＿＿＿＿＿＿＿＿＿＿＿＿＿

＿＿＿＿＿＿＿＿＿＿＿＿＿＿＿＿＿＿＿＿＿＿＿

20＿＿ * ＿＿＿＿＿＿＿＿＿＿＿＿＿＿＿＿＿＿

＿＿＿＿＿＿＿＿＿＿＿＿＿＿＿＿＿＿＿＿＿＿＿

＿＿＿＿＿＿＿＿＿＿＿＿＿＿＿＿＿＿＿＿＿＿＿

20＿＿ * ＿＿＿＿＿＿＿＿＿＿＿＿＿＿＿＿＿＿

＿＿＿＿＿＿＿＿＿＿＿＿＿＿＿＿＿＿＿＿＿＿＿

＿＿＿＿＿＿＿＿＿＿＿＿＿＿＿＿＿＿＿＿＿＿＿

APRIL 26

The worst or oddest gift I received
recently was . . . , from . . .

20 __ __ ✳ _____

_____

_____

20 __ __ ✳ _____

_____

_____

20 __ __ ✳ _____

_____

_____

20 __ __ ✳ _____

_____

_____

20 __ __ ✳ _____

_____

_____

APRIL 27

My favorite creative outlet is . . .

20_____ _____ * _____

_____

_____

_____

20_____ _____ * _____

_____

_____

_____

20_____ _____ * _____

_____

_____

_____

20_____ _____ * _____

_____

_____

_____

20_____ _____ * _____

_____

_____

_____

APRIL 28

My ideal morning would be to . . .

20__ __ * _____

_____

_____

|||||||||||||||||||||||||||||||||||||||||||||||||||||||||||||||||||||||||||||||

20__ __ * _____

_____

_____

|||||||||||||||||||||||||||||||||||||||||||||||||||||||||||||||||||||||||||||||

20__ __ * _____

_____

_____

|||||||||||||||||||||||||||||||||||||||||||||||||||||||||||||||||||||||||||||||

20__ __ * _____

_____

_____

|||||||||||||||||||||||||||||||||||||||||||||||||||||||||||||||||||||||||||||||

20__ __ * _____

_____

_____

|||||||||||||||||||||||||||||||||||||||||||||||||||||||||||||||||||||||||||||||

If I could be a supernatural creature, I would be a . . .

20___ ___ * _____

_____

_____

20___ ___ * _____

_____

_____

20___ ___ * _____

_____

_____

20___ ___ * _____

_____

_____

20___ ___ * _____

_____

_____

APRIL 30

The mode of transportation I use most often is . . .

20___ ___ * _____

_____

_____

20___ ___ * _____

_____

_____

20___ ___ * _____

_____

_____

20___ ___ * _____

_____

_____

20___ ___ * _____

_____

_____

MAY 1

From a scale of 1 to 10, my energy level today is . . .

20___ ___ * _____

_____

_____

||||||||||||||||||||||||||||||||||||||||||||||||||||||||||||||||||||||||||||||||||||||

20___ ___ * _____

_____

_____

||||||||||||||||||||||||||||||||||||||||||||||||||||||||||||||||||||||||||||||||||||||

20___ ___ * _____

_____

_____

||||||||||||||||||||||||||||||||||||||||||||||||||||||||||||||||||||||||||||||||||||||

20___ ___ * _____

_____

_____

||||||||||||||||||||||||||||||||||||||||||||||||||||||||||||||||||||||||||||||||||||||

20___ ___ * _____

_____

_____

||||||||||||||||||||||||||||||||||||||||||||||||||||||||||||||||||||||||||||||||||||||

MAY 2

The last thing I bought online was . . .

20___ ___ * _____

_____

_____

_____

20___ ___ * _____

_____

_____

_____

20___ ___ * _____

_____

_____

_____

20___ ___ * _____

_____

_____

_____

20___ ___ * _____

_____

_____

_____

MAY 3

If I went to get a tattoo today it would be of . . . because . . .

20 __ __ * _____

_____

_____

_____

20 __ __ * _____

_____

_____

_____

20 __ __ * _____

_____

_____

_____

20 __ __ * _____

_____

_____

_____

20 __ __ * _____

_____

_____

_____

MAY 4

The number one song on my playlist these days is . . .

20___ ___ * _____

_____

_____

20___ ___ * _____

_____

_____

20___ ___ * _____

_____

_____

20___ ___ * _____

_____

_____

20___ ___ * _____

_____

_____

MAY 5

If I could change one thing about my body it would be . . .

20___ ___ * _____

_____

_____

_____

20___ ___ * _____

_____

_____

_____

20___ ___ * _____

_____

_____

_____

20___ ___ * _____

_____

_____

_____

20___ ___ * _____

_____

_____

_____

MAY 6

The best age to be is . . . because . . .

20 __ __ * _____

_____

_____

_____

20 __ __ * _____

_____

_____

_____

20 __ __ * _____

_____

_____

_____

20 __ __ * _____

_____

_____

_____

20 __ __ * _____

_____

_____

_____

MAY 7

I would love to undertake a project about . . .

20___ ___ * _____

_____

_____

_____

20___ ___ * _____

_____

_____

_____

20___ ___ * _____

_____

_____

_____

20___ ___ * _____

_____

_____

_____

20___ ___ * _____

_____

_____

_____

MAY 8

My favorite flavor of ice cream is . . .

20___ ___ * _____

_____

_____

_____

20___ ___ * _____

_____

_____

_____

20___ ___ * _____

_____

_____

_____

20___ ___ * _____

_____

_____

_____

20___ ___ * _____

_____

_____

_____

MAY 9

I would have loved to have been in . . . when . . . happened.

20__ __ * _____

_____

_____

20__ __ * _____

_____

_____

20__ __ * _____

_____

_____

20__ __ * _____

_____

_____

20__ __ * _____

_____

_____

MAY 10

This year when . . . it was a blessing in disguise.

20___ ___ * _____

_____

_____

20___ ___ * _____

_____

_____

20___ ___ * _____

_____

_____

20___ ___ * _____

_____

_____

20___ ___ * _____

_____

_____

MAY 11

I think the coolest first name for a girl is . . .

20___ ___ * _____

_____

_____

_____

20___ ___ * _____

_____

_____

_____

20___ ___ * _____

_____

_____

_____

20___ ___ * _____

_____

_____

_____

20___ ___ * _____

_____

_____

_____

MAY 12

I think the coolest first name for a boy is . . .

20___ ___ * _____

_____

_____

20___ ___ * _____

_____

_____

20___ ___ * _____

_____

_____

20___ ___ * _____

_____

_____

20___ ___ * _____

_____

_____

MAY 13

It felt like déjà vu when . . .

20___ ___ * _____

_____

_____

20___ ___ * _____

_____

_____

20___ ___ * _____

_____

_____

20___ ___ * _____

_____

_____

20___ ___ * _____

_____

_____

MAY 14

*If I could hang out with a singer, musician,
or band, it would have to be . . .*

20 __ __ * _____

_____

_____

20 __ __ * _____

_____

_____

20 __ __ * _____

_____

_____

20 __ __ * _____

_____

_____

20 __ __ * _____

_____

_____

MAY 15

If I could own a business, it would be . . .

20___ ___ * _____

_____

_____

20___ ___ * _____

_____

_____

20___ ___ * _____

_____

_____

20___ ___ * _____

_____

_____

20___ ___ * _____

_____

_____

MAY 16

I wish I knew that . . . this time last year.

20 __ __ * _____

_____

_____

|||||||||||||||||||||||||||||||||||||||||||||||||||||||||||||||||

20 __ __ * _____

_____

_____

|||||||||||||||||||||||||||||||||||||||||||||||||||||||||||||||||

20 __ __ * _____

_____

_____

|||||||||||||||||||||||||||||||||||||||||||||||||||||||||||||||||

20 __ __ * _____

_____

_____

|||||||||||||||||||||||||||||||||||||||||||||||||||||||||||||||||

20 __ __ * _____

_____

_____

|||||||||||||||||||||||||||||||||||||||||||||||||||||||||||||||||

MAY 17

Before I fell asleep last night, I was thinking about . . .

20___ ___ * _____

_____

_____

20___ ___ * _____

_____

_____

20___ ___ * _____

_____

_____

20___ ___ * _____

_____

_____

20___ ___ * _____

_____

_____

The most dangerous or riskiest thing I did this year was . . .

20 __ __ * _____

_____

_____

20 __ __ * _____

_____

_____

20 __ __ * _____

_____

_____

20 __ __ * _____

_____

_____

20 __ __ * _____

_____

_____

MAY 19

The musical instrument I wish I could play is . . .

20___ ___ * _____

_____

_____

20___ ___ * _____

_____

_____

20___ ___ * _____

_____

_____

20___ ___ * _____

_____

_____

20___ ___ * _____

_____

_____

MAY 20

Right now I can hear . . .

20___ ___ * _____

_____

_____

_____

20___ ___ * _____

_____

_____

_____

20___ ___ * _____

_____

_____

_____

20___ ___ * _____

_____

_____

_____

20___ ___ * _____

_____

_____

_____

MAY 21

The most annoying person I have to interact with is . . .

20___ ___ * _____

_____

_____

20___ ___ * _____

_____

_____

20___ ___ * _____

_____

_____

20___ ___ * _____

_____

_____

20___ ___ * _____

_____

_____

MAY 22

The last person I talked to was . . .

20 __ __ * _____

_____

_____

|||||||||||||||||||||||||||||||||||||||||||||||||||||||||||||||||||||||||||||||||||||||||||||||||||||||||||||||

20 __ __ * _____

_____

_____

|||||||||||||||||||||||||||||||||||||||||||||||||||||||||||||||||||||||||||||||||||||||||||||||||||||||||||||||

20 __ __ * _____

_____

_____

|||||||||||||||||||||||||||||||||||||||||||||||||||||||||||||||||||||||||||||||||||||||||||||||||||||||||||||||

20 __ __ * _____

_____

_____

|||||||||||||||||||||||||||||||||||||||||||||||||||||||||||||||||||||||||||||||||||||||||||||||||||||||||||||||

20 __ __ * _____

_____

_____

|||||||||||||||||||||||||||||||||||||||||||||||||||||||||||||||||||||||||||||||||||||||||||||||||||||||||||||||

MAY 23

My dream car would be . . .

20___ ___ * _____

_____

_____

_____

20___ ___ * _____

_____

_____

_____

20___ ___ * _____

_____

_____

_____

20___ ___ * _____

_____

_____

_____

20___ ___ * _____

_____

_____

_____

MAY 24

If I could be in the Olympics,
I would compete in the sport of . . .

20___ ___ * _____

_____

_____

20___ ___ * _____

_____

_____

20___ ___ * _____

_____

_____

20___ ___ * _____

_____

_____

_____

20___ ___ * _____

_____

_____

MAY 25

The person I know with the best sense of humor is . . .

20___ ___ * _____

_____

_____

20___ ___ * _____

_____

_____

20___ ___ * _____

_____

_____

20___ ___ * _____

_____

_____

20___ ___ * _____

_____

_____

MAY 26

The person in my life I most enjoy
spending time with is . . .

20 __ __ * _____

_____

_____

_____

20 __ __ * _____

_____

_____

_____

20 __ __ * _____

_____

_____

_____

20 __ __ * _____

_____

_____

_____

20 __ __ * _____

_____

_____

_____

MAY 27

The last time I went a little wild and crazy was when . . .

20___ ___ * _____

_____

_____

20___ ___ * _____

_____

_____

20___ ___ * _____

_____

_____

20___ ___ * _____

_____

_____

20___ ___ * _____

_____

_____

MAY 28

My first thought of the day was about . . .

20 __ __ * _____

_____

_____

_____

20 __ __ * _____

_____

_____

_____

20 __ __ * _____

_____

_____

_____

20 __ __ * _____

_____

_____

_____

20 __ __ * _____

_____

_____

_____

MAY 29

The most unusual person I have met recently is . . .

20___ ___ * _____

_____

_____

_____

20___ ___ * _____

_____

_____

_____

20___ ___ * _____

_____

_____

_____

20___ ___ * _____

_____

_____

_____

20___ ___ * _____

_____

_____

_____

MAY 30

The most embarrassing thing that happened lately was . . .

20 __ __ * _____

_____

_____

_____

20 __ __ * _____

_____

_____

_____

20 __ __ * _____

_____

_____

_____

20 __ __ * _____

_____

_____

_____

20 __ __ * _____

_____

_____

_____

If I could have a dual passport, the other country I
would choose to be a citizen of would be . . .

20 __ __ * _____

_____

_____

_____

20 __ __ * _____

_____

_____

_____

20 __ __ * _____

_____

_____

_____

20 __ __ * _____

_____

_____

_____

20 __ __ * _____

_____

_____

_____

JUNE 1

If I could put a message in a time capsule for
future generations it would say . . .

20___ ___ * _____

_____

_____

20___ ___ * _____

_____

_____

20___ ___ * _____

_____

_____

20___ ___ * _____

_____

_____

20___ ___ * _____

_____

_____

JUNE 2

I would like to be able to tell . . . about . . .

20___ ___ * _____

_____

_____

_____

||||||||||||||||||||||||||||||||||||||||||||||||||||||||||||||||||||||||||||||||||||||||||||||||||||||||||

20___ ___ * _____

_____

_____

_____

||||||||||||||||||||||||||||||||||||||||||||||||||||||||||||||||||||||||||||||||||||||||||||||||||||||||||

20___ ___ * _____

_____

_____

_____

||||||||||||||||||||||||||||||||||||||||||||||||||||||||||||||||||||||||||||||||||||||||||||||||||||||||||

20___ ___ * _____

_____

_____

_____

||||||||||||||||||||||||||||||||||||||||||||||||||||||||||||||||||||||||||||||||||||||||||||||||||||||||||

20___ ___ * _____

_____

_____

_____

||||||||||||||||||||||||||||||||||||||||||||||||||||||||||||||||||||||||||||||||||||||||||||||||||||||||||

JUNE 3

The biggest lesson I learned this year was that . . .

20 _ _ * _____

_____

_____

_____

20 _ _ * _____

_____

_____

_____

20 _ _ * _____

_____

_____

_____

20 _ _ * _____

_____

_____

_____

20 _ _ * _____

_____

_____

_____

JUNE 4

The last person I kissed was . . .

20___ ___ ✳ _____

_____

_____

20___ ___ ✳ _____

_____

_____

20___ ___ ✳ _____

_____

_____

20___ ___ ✳ _____

_____

_____

20___ ___ ✳ _____

_____

_____

JUNE 5

I feel sorry for . . .

20__ __ * _____

_____

_____

_____

20__ __ * _____

_____

_____

_____

20__ __ * _____

_____

_____

_____

20__ __ * _____

_____

_____

_____

20__ __ * _____

_____

_____

_____

JUNE 6

The best holiday I had this year was . . .

20___ ___ * _____

_____

_____

||||||||||||||||||||||||||||||||||||||||||||||||||||||||||||||||||||||||||||||||||||||||||||||||||||||||||||||||||||||

20___ ___ * _____

_____

_____

||||||||||||||||||||||||||||||||||||||||||||||||||||||||||||||||||||||||||||||||||||||||||||||||||||||||||||||||||||||

20___ ___ * _____

_____

_____

||||||||||||||||||||||||||||||||||||||||||||||||||||||||||||||||||||||||||||||||||||||||||||||||||||||||||||||||||||||

20___ ___ * _____

_____

_____

||||||||||||||||||||||||||||||||||||||||||||||||||||||||||||||||||||||||||||||||||||||||||||||||||||||||||||||||||||||

20___ ___ * _____

_____

_____

||||||||||||||||||||||||||||||||||||||||||||||||||||||||||||||||||||||||||||||||||||||||||||||||||||||||||||||||||||||

JUNE 7

The worst holiday I had this year was . . .

20___ ___ * _____

_____

_____

20___ ___ * _____

_____

_____

20___ ___ * _____

_____

_____

20___ ___ * _____

_____

_____

20___ ___ * _____

_____

_____

JUNE 8

If I could be reincarnated, I would come back as . . .

20___ ___ * _____

_____

_____

|||||||||||||||||||||||||||||||||||||||||||||||||||||||||||||||||||||||||||||||||||||||||||||||||||||||

20___ ___ * _____

_____

_____

|||||||||||||||||||||||||||||||||||||||||||||||||||||||||||||||||||||||||||||||||||||||||||||||||||||||

20___ ___ * _____

_____

_____

|||||||||||||||||||||||||||||||||||||||||||||||||||||||||||||||||||||||||||||||||||||||||||||||||||||||

20___ ___ * _____

_____

_____

|||||||||||||||||||||||||||||||||||||||||||||||||||||||||||||||||||||||||||||||||||||||||||||||||||||||

20___ ___ * _____

_____

_____

|||||||||||||||||||||||||||||||||||||||||||||||||||||||||||||||||||||||||||||||||||||||||||||||||||||||

JUNE 9

I am most attracted to . . .

20___ ___ * _____

_____

_____

20___ ___ * _____

_____

_____

20___ ___ * _____

_____

_____

20___ ___ * _____

_____

_____

20___ ___ * _____

_____

_____

JUNE 10

I am kind of grossed out by . . .

20__ __ * _____
_____
_____
_____

20__ __ * _____
_____
_____
_____

20__ __ * _____
_____
_____
_____

20__ __ * _____
_____
_____
_____

20__ __ * _____
_____
_____
_____

JUNE 11

. . . had a big influence on me this year.

20__ __ * _____

_____

_____

20__ __ * _____

_____

_____

20__ __ * _____

_____

_____

20__ __ * _____

_____

_____

20__ __ * _____

_____

_____

_____

JUNE 12

In my family, . . . is the one I talk to the most.

20__ __ * _____
_____
_____

20__ __ * _____
_____
_____

20__ __ * _____
_____
_____

20__ __ * _____
_____
_____

20__ __ * _____
_____
_____

JUNE 13

*The most life-changing, pivotal moment
of the year for me was . . .*

20___ ___ * _____

_____

_____

_____

20___ ___ * _____

_____

_____

_____

20___ ___ * _____

_____

_____

_____

20___ ___ * _____

_____

_____

_____

20___ ___ * _____

_____

_____

_____

If I could write a memoir, it would be called . . .

20 __ __ * _____

_____

_____

_____

20 __ __ * _____

_____

_____

_____

20 __ __ * _____

_____

_____

_____

20 __ __ * _____

_____

_____

_____

20 __ __ * _____

_____

_____

_____

The time I recently felt the most beautiful/handsome was . . .

20 __ __ * _____

_____

_____

_____

20 __ __ * _____

_____

_____

_____

20 __ __ * _____

_____

_____

_____

20 __ __ * _____

_____

_____

_____

20 __ __ * _____

_____

_____

_____

If I could throw a party, no expenses spared,
it would be in . . . , with . . .

20__ __ * _____

_____

_____

20__ __ * _____

_____

_____

20__ __ * _____

_____

_____

20__ __ * _____

_____

_____

20__ __ * _____

_____

_____

JUNE 17

My biggest gripe right now is . . .

20 __ __ * _____

_____

_____

_____

20 __ __ * _____

_____

_____

_____

20 __ __ * _____

_____

_____

_____

20 __ __ * _____

_____

_____

_____

20 __ __ * _____

_____

_____

_____

JUNE 18

Last night I slept . . .

20___ ___ ✳ _____

_____

_____

_____

20___ ___ ✳ _____

_____

_____

_____

20___ ___ ✳ _____

_____

_____

_____

20___ ___ ✳ _____

_____

_____

_____

20___ ___ ✳ _____

_____

_____

_____

JUNE 19

When I heard in the news that . . . I felt very moved.

20__ __ * _____

_____

_____

_____

20__ __ * _____

_____

_____

_____

20__ __ * _____

_____

_____

_____

20__ __ * _____

_____

_____

_____

20__ __ * _____

_____

_____

_____

If I had nine lives, I would master . . .

20___ ___ * _____

_____

_____

||||||||||||||||||||||||||||||||||||||||||||||||||||||||||||||||||||||||||||||||||||

20___ ___ * _____

_____

_____

||||||||||||||||||||||||||||||||||||||||||||||||||||||||||||||||||||||||||||||||||||

20___ ___ * _____

_____

_____

||||||||||||||||||||||||||||||||||||||||||||||||||||||||||||||||||||||||||||||||||||

20___ ___ * _____

_____

_____

||||||||||||||||||||||||||||||||||||||||||||||||||||||||||||||||||||||||||||||||||||

20___ ___ * _____

_____

_____

||||||||||||||||||||||||||||||||||||||||||||||||||||||||||||||||||||||||||||||||||||

JUNE 21

The biggest fear I recently overcame was . . .

20___ ___ * _____

_____

_____

20___ ___ * _____

_____

_____

20___ ___ * _____

_____

_____

20___ ___ * _____

_____

_____

20___ ___ * _____

_____

_____

JUNE 22

The biggest hurdle I recently overcame was . . .

20___ ___ * _____

_____

_____

_____

20___ ___ * _____

_____

_____

_____

20___ ___ * _____

_____

_____

_____

20___ ___ * _____

_____

_____

_____

20___ ___ * _____

_____

_____

_____

JUNE 23

My favorite actor on television is . . .

20___ ___ ✳ _____

_____

_____

20___ ___ ✳ _____

_____

_____

20___ ___ ✳ _____

_____

_____

20___ ___ ✳ _____

_____

_____

20___ ___ ✳ _____

_____

_____

JUNE 24

If I could have a foreign accent, it would be . . .

20___ ___ * _____

_____

_____

|||||||||||||||||||||||||||||||||||||||||||||||||||||||||||||||||||||||||||||||||||||||||||||

20___ ___ * _____

_____

_____

|||||||||||||||||||||||||||||||||||||||||||||||||||||||||||||||||||||||||||||||||||||||||||||

20___ ___ * _____

_____

_____

|||||||||||||||||||||||||||||||||||||||||||||||||||||||||||||||||||||||||||||||||||||||||||||

20___ ___ * _____

_____

_____

|||||||||||||||||||||||||||||||||||||||||||||||||||||||||||||||||||||||||||||||||||||||||||||

20___ ___ * _____

_____

_____

|||||||||||||||||||||||||||||||||||||||||||||||||||||||||||||||||||||||||||||||||||||||||||||

JUNE 25

My least-liked chore to do is . . .

20___ ___ * _____

_____

_____

20___ ___ * _____

_____

_____

20___ ___ * _____

_____

_____

20___ ___ * _____

_____

_____

20___ ___ * _____

_____

_____

My favorite café or restaurant is . . .

20___ ___ * _____

_____

_____

_____

20___ ___ * _____

_____

_____

_____

20___ ___ * _____

_____

_____

_____

20___ ___ * _____

_____

_____

_____

20___ ___ * _____

_____

_____

_____

JUNE 27

The worst meal I had recently was . . .

20___ ___ * _____

_____

_____

20___ ___ * _____

_____

_____

20___ ___ * _____

_____

_____

20___ ___ * _____

_____

_____

20___ ___ * _____

_____

_____

JUNE 28

One thing I am not very good at is . . .

20 __ __ * _____

_____

_____

|||||||||||||||||||||||||||||||||||||||||||||||||||||||||||||||||||||||||

20 __ __ * _____

_____

_____

|||||||||||||||||||||||||||||||||||||||||||||||||||||||||||||||||||||||||

20 __ __ * _____

_____

_____

|||||||||||||||||||||||||||||||||||||||||||||||||||||||||||||||||||||||||

20 __ __ * _____

_____

_____

|||||||||||||||||||||||||||||||||||||||||||||||||||||||||||||||||||||||||

20 __ __ * _____

_____

_____

|||||||||||||||||||||||||||||||||||||||||||||||||||||||||||||||||||||||||

JUNE 29

I would never . . .

20___ ___ * _____

_____

_____

20___ ___ * _____

_____

_____

20___ ___ * _____

_____

_____

20___ ___ * _____

_____

_____

20___ ___ * _____

_____

_____

JUNE 30

The last time I saw the ocean was . . .

20___ ___ * _____

_____

_____

20___ ___ * _____

_____

_____

20___ ___ * _____

_____

_____

20___ ___ * _____

_____

_____

20___ ___ * _____

_____

_____

JULY 1

The greatest sense of contentment
I experienced recently was . . .

20___ ___ * _____

_____

_____

20___ ___ * _____

_____

_____

20___ ___ * _____

_____

_____

20___ ___ * _____

_____

_____

20___ ___ * _____

_____

_____

JULY 2

The most stressed I have been recently was when . . .

20___ ___ * _____

_____

_____

_____

20___ ___ * _____

_____

_____

_____

20___ ___ * _____

_____

_____

_____

20___ ___ * _____

_____

_____

_____

20___ ___ * _____

_____

_____

_____

JULY 3

The amount of time I was online today was . . .

20___ ___ * _____

_____

_____

20___ ___ * _____

_____

_____

20___ ___ * _____

_____

_____

20___ ___ * _____

_____

_____

20___ ___ * _____

_____

_____

JULY 4

The daily thing I have to do that I enjoy most is . . . . .

20___ ___ * _____

_____

_____

20___ ___ * _____

_____

_____

20___ ___ * _____

_____

_____

20___ ___ * _____

_____

_____

20___ ___ * _____

_____

_____

JULY 5

The daily thing I have to do that I enjoy least is . . . . .

20___ ___ * _____

_____

_____

_____

20___ ___ * _____

_____

_____

_____

20___ ___ * _____

_____

_____

_____

20___ ___ * _____

_____

_____

_____

20___ ___ * _____

_____

_____

_____

JULY 6

. . . and . . . and . . . are on my night table.

20___ ___ * _____

_____

_____

_____

20___ ___ * _____

_____

_____

_____

20___ ___ * _____

_____

_____

_____

20___ ___ * _____

_____

_____

_____

20___ ___ * _____

_____

_____

_____

JULY 7

My favorite thing to drink is . . .

20___ ___ * _____

_____

_____

_____

20___ ___ * _____

_____

_____

_____

20___ ___ * _____

_____

_____

_____

20___ ___ * _____

_____

_____

_____

20___ ___ * _____

_____

_____

_____

JULY 8

If I had the whole afternoon to do as I please,
the first thing I would do is . . .

20__ __ * _____

_____

_____

20__ __ * _____

_____

_____

20__ __ * _____

_____

_____

20__ __ * _____

_____

_____

20__ __ * _____

_____

_____

JULY 9

I cannot understand why . . . is famous.

20___ ___ * _____

_____

_____

20___ ___ * _____

_____

_____

20___ ___ * _____

_____

_____

20___ ___ * _____

_____

_____

20___ ___ * _____

_____

_____

JULY 10

My favorite area of my home is . . .

20___ ___ * _____

_____

_____

|||||||||||||||||||||||||||||||||||||||||||||||||||||||||||||||||||||||||||||||

20___ ___ * _____

_____

_____

|||||||||||||||||||||||||||||||||||||||||||||||||||||||||||||||||||||||||||||||

20___ ___ * _____

_____

_____

|||||||||||||||||||||||||||||||||||||||||||||||||||||||||||||||||||||||||||||||

20___ ___ * _____

_____

_____

|||||||||||||||||||||||||||||||||||||||||||||||||||||||||||||||||||||||||||||||

20___ ___ * _____

_____

_____

|||||||||||||||||||||||||||||||||||||||||||||||||||||||||||||||||||||||||||||||

JULY 11

If I could renovate an area of my home it would be the . . .

20 __ __ * _____

_____

_____

20 __ __ * _____

_____

_____

20 __ __ *⁎ _____

_____

_____

20 __ __ * _____

_____

_____

20 __ __ * _____

_____

_____

JULY 12

The type of cuisine I eat the most is . . .

20___ ___ * _____

_____

_____

||||||||||||||||||||||||||||||||||||||||||||||||||||||||||||||||||||||||||||||||||||||||

20___ ___ * _____

_____

_____

||||||||||||||||||||||||||||||||||||||||||||||||||||||||||||||||||||||||||||||||||||||||

20___ ___ * _____

_____

_____

||||||||||||||||||||||||||||||||||||||||||||||||||||||||||||||||||||||||||||||||||||||||

20___ ___ * _____

_____

_____

||||||||||||||||||||||||||||||||||||||||||||||||||||||||||||||||||||||||||||||||||||||||

20___ ___ * _____

_____

_____

||||||||||||||||||||||||||||||||||||||||||||||||||||||||||||||||||||||||||||||||||||||||

JULY 13

If I could go back to school, I would major in . . .

20__ __ * _____

_____

_____

20__ __ * _____

_____

_____

20__ __ * _____

_____

_____

20__ __ * _____

_____

_____

20__ __ * _____

_____

_____

JULY 14

The most recent coincidence I experienced was . . .

20__ __ * _____

_____

_____

20__ __ * _____

_____

_____

20__ __ * _____

_____

_____

20__ __ * _____

_____

_____

20__ __ * _____

_____

_____

JULY 15

A saying I am always quoting is . . .

20___ ___ * _____

_____

_____

_____

20___ ___ * _____

_____

_____

_____

20___ ___ * _____

_____

_____

_____

20___ ___ * _____

_____

_____

_____

20___ ___ * _____

_____

_____

_____

JULY 16

The last person to show up in my doorway was . . .

20___ ___ * _____
_____
_____
_____

20___ ___ * _____
_____
_____
_____

20___ ___ * _____
_____
_____
_____

20___ ___ * _____
_____
_____
_____

20___ ___ * _____
_____
_____
_____

JULY 17

The most expensive thing I own is . . .

20___ ___ * _____
_____
_____
_____

20___ ___ * _____
_____
_____
_____

20___ ___ * _____
_____
_____
_____

20___ ___ * _____
_____
_____
_____

20___ ___ * _____
_____
_____
_____

JULY 18

My favorite part of the city or town I live in is . . .

20___ ___ * _____

_____

_____

20___ ___ * _____

_____

_____

20___ ___ * _____

_____

_____

20___ ___ * _____

_____

_____

20___ ___ * _____

_____

_____

JULY 19

The worst thing about the city or town I live in is . . .

20__ __ * _____

_____

_____

|||||||||||||||||||||||||||||||||||||||||||||||||||||||||||||||||||||||

20__ __ * _____

_____

_____

|||||||||||||||||||||||||||||||||||||||||||||||||||||||||||||||||||||||

20__ __ * _____

_____

_____

|||||||||||||||||||||||||||||||||||||||||||||||||||||||||||||||||||||||

20__ __ * _____

_____

_____

|||||||||||||||||||||||||||||||||||||||||||||||||||||||||||||||||||||||

20__ __ * _____

_____

_____

|||||||||||||||||||||||||||||||||||||||||||||||||||||||||||||||||||||||

If I could give a big donation
to any charity, it would be . . .

20__ __ * _____

20__ __ * _____

20__ __ * _____

20__ __ * _____

20__ __ * _____

JULY 21

The smartest person I know is . . .

20___ ___ * _____

_____

_____

20___ ___ * _____

_____

_____

20___ ___ * _____

_____

_____

20___ ___ * _____

_____

_____

20___ ___ * _____

_____

_____

JULY 22

The last time I took a nap was . . .

20___ ___ * _____
_____
_____

20___ ___ * _____
_____
_____

20___ ___ * _____
_____
_____

20___ ___ * _____
_____
_____

20___ ___ * _____
_____
_____

JULY 23

The theme song to my life is . . .

20__ __ * _____

_____

_____

20__ __ * _____

_____

_____

20__ __ * _____

_____

_____

20__ __ * _____

_____

_____

20__ __ * _____

_____

_____

JULY 24

The last e-mail I sent was to . . .

20_____ * _____

_____

_____

_____

20_____ * _____

_____

_____

_____

20_____ * _____

_____

_____

_____

20_____ * _____

_____

_____

_____

20_____ * _____

_____

_____

_____

The last envelope I mailed was sent to . . .

20___ ___ * _____

_____

_____

20___ ___ * _____

_____

_____

20___ ___ * _____

_____

_____

20___ ___ * _____

_____

_____

20___ ___ * _____

_____

_____

JULY 26

If I found a genie in a bottle, I would
ask for these three wishes: . . .

20__ __ * _____

_____

_____

_____

20__ __ * _____

_____

_____

_____

20__ __ * _____

_____

_____

_____

20__ __ * _____

_____

_____

_____

20__ __ * _____

_____

_____

_____

JULY 27

I have a little OCD about . . .

20___ ___ ＊ _____

_____

_____

20___ ___ ＊ _____

_____

_____

20___ ___ ＊ _____

_____

_____

20___ ___ ＊ _____

_____

_____

20___ ___ ＊ _____

_____

_____

JULY 28

This year I acted as a mentor to . . .

20___ ___ * _____
_____
_____
_____

20___ ___ * _____
_____
_____
_____

20___ ___ * _____
_____
_____
_____

20___ ___ * _____
_____
_____
_____

20___ ___ * _____
_____
_____
_____

JULY 29

*An Oscar-nominated film I saw
in a theater this year was . . .*

20____ ____ * _____

_____

_____

20____ ____ * _____

_____

_____

20____ ____ * _____

_____

_____

20____ ____ * _____

_____

_____

20____ ____ * _____

_____

_____

JULY 30

I wish my phone had an app that would . . .

20___ ___ * _____

_____

_____

_____

20___ ___ * _____

_____

_____

_____

20___ ___ * _____

_____

_____

_____

20___ ___ * _____

_____

_____

_____

20___ ___ * _____

_____

_____

_____

JULY 31

I think the celebrity with the best hair is . . .

20___ ___ * _____

_____

_____

_____

20___ ___ * _____

_____

_____

_____

20___ ___ * _____

_____

_____

_____

20___ ___ * _____

_____

_____

_____

20___ ___ * _____

_____

_____

_____

AUGUST 1

*My satisfaction with my current weight
on a scale of 1 to 10 is . . .*

20___ ___ * _____

_____

_____

_____

20___ ___ * _____

_____

_____

_____

20___ ___ * _____

_____

_____

_____

20___ ___ * _____

_____

_____

_____

20___ ___ * _____

_____

_____

_____

AUGUST 2

The most mischievous thing I did recently was . . .

20___ ___ * _____

_____

_____

20___ ___ * _____

_____

_____

20___ ___ * _____

_____

_____

20___ ___ * _____

_____

_____

20___ ___ * _____

_____

_____

AUGUST 3

My favorite city in the world is . . .

20___ ___ * _____
_____
_____
|||||||||||||||||||||||||||||||||||||||||||||||||||||||||||||||||||||||||||||||||||||||||||||||||||

20___ ___ * _____
_____
_____
|||||||||||||||||||||||||||||||||||||||||||||||||||||||||||||||||||||||||||||||||||||||||||||||||||

20___ ___ * _____
_____
_____
|||||||||||||||||||||||||||||||||||||||||||||||||||||||||||||||||||||||||||||||||||||||||||||||||||

20___ ___ * _____
_____
_____
|||||||||||||||||||||||||||||||||||||||||||||||||||||||||||||||||||||||||||||||||||||||||||||||||||

20___ ___ * _____
_____
_____
|||||||||||||||||||||||||||||||||||||||||||||||||||||||||||||||||||||||||||||||||||||||||||||||||||

AUGUST 4

My least favorite city in the world is . . .

20___ ___ * _____

_____

_____

_____

20___ ___ * _____

_____

_____

_____

20___ ___ * _____

_____

_____

_____

20___ ___ * _____

_____

_____

_____

20___ ___ * _____

_____

_____

_____

AUGUST 5

The last time I went to the gym or worked out was . . .

20__ __ * _____

_____

_____

20__ __ * _____

_____

_____

20__ __ * _____

_____

_____

20__ __ * _____

_____

_____

20__ __ * _____

_____

_____

The most alive I have felt recently is when . . . . .

20___ ___ * _____

_____

_____

_____

20___ ___ * _____

_____

_____

_____

20___ ___ * _____

_____

_____

_____

20___ ___ * _____

_____

_____

_____

20___ ___ * _____

_____

_____

_____

AUGUST 7

I watched . . . hours of television yesterday.

20___ ___ * _____

_____

_____

_____

20___ ___ * _____

_____

_____

_____

20___ ___ * _____

_____

_____

_____

20___ ___ * _____

_____

_____

_____

20___ ___ * _____

_____

_____

_____

AUGUST 8

I am proud to be a citizen of my country because . . .

20____ ____ * _____

_____

_____

_____

20____ ____ * _____

_____

_____

_____

20____ ____ * _____

_____

_____

_____

20____ ____ * _____

_____

_____

_____

20____ ____ * _____

_____

_____

_____

AUGUST 9

One thing I wish the government in
my country would not do is . . .

20___ ___ * _____

_____

_____

20___ ___ * _____

_____

_____

20___ ___ * _____

_____

_____

20___ ___ * _____

_____

_____

20___ ___ * _____

_____

_____

AUGUST 10

*If I could invite three fictional characters
to a dinner party, they would be . . . . .*

20___ ___ * _____

_____

_____

_____

20___ ___ * _____

_____

_____

_____

20___ ___ * _____

_____

_____

_____

20___ ___ * _____

_____

_____

_____

20___ ___ * _____

_____

_____

_____

AUGUST 11

The last person's advice I followed was . . . to . . .

20__ __ * _____

_____

_____

_____

20__ __ * _____

_____

_____

_____

20__ __ * _____

_____

_____

_____

20__ __ * _____

_____

_____

_____

20__ __ * _____

_____

_____

_____

AUGUST 12

The friend I miss most whom
I have not seen in a while is . . .

20___ ___ ＊ _____

_____

_____

_____

20___ ___ ＊ _____

_____

_____

_____

20___ ___ ＊ _____

_____

_____

_____

20___ ___ ＊ _____

_____

_____

_____

20___ ___ ＊ _____

_____

_____

_____

AUGUST 13

The friend I hang out with most lately is . . .

20___ ___ * _____

_____

_____

20___ ___ * _____

_____

_____

20___ ___ * _____

_____

_____

20___ ___ * _____

_____

_____

20___ ___ * _____

_____

_____

AUGUST 14

The last live show I saw was . . .

20___ ___ * _____

_____

_____

20___ ___ * _____

_____

_____

20___ ___ * _____

_____

_____

20___ ___ * _____

_____

_____

20___ ___ * _____

_____

_____

AUGUST 15

The last argument I had was with . . . about . . .

20___ ___ * _____

_____

_____

20___ ___ * _____

_____

_____

20___ ___ * _____

_____

_____

20___ ___ * _____

_____

_____

20___ ___ * _____

_____

_____

AUGUST 16

My most prized heirloom is . . .

20___ ___ * _____

_____

_____

_____

20___ ___ * _____

_____

_____

_____

20___ ___ * _____

_____

_____

_____

20___ ___ * _____

_____

_____

_____

20___ ___ * _____

_____

_____

_____

AUGUST 17

I most recently acted as a good Samaritan when I . . .

20___ ___ * _____

_____

_____

||||||||||||||||||||||||||||||||||||||||||||||||||||||||||||||||||||||||||||||||||||||||||

20___ ___ * _____

_____

_____

||||||||||||||||||||||||||||||||||||||||||||||||||||||||||||||||||||||||||||||||||||||||||

20___ ___ * _____

_____

_____

||||||||||||||||||||||||||||||||||||||||||||||||||||||||||||||||||||||||||||||||||||||||||

20___ ___ * _____

_____

_____

||||||||||||||||||||||||||||||||||||||||||||||||||||||||||||||||||||||||||||||||||||||||||

20___ ___ * _____

_____

_____

||||||||||||||||||||||||||||||||||||||||||||||||||||||||||||||||||||||||||||||||||||||||||

AUGUST 18

If I could plan an extended trip around the world, my itinerary would include . . .

20 __ __ * _____

_____

_____

20 __ __ * _____

_____

_____

20 __ __ * _____

_____

_____

20 __ __ * _____

_____

_____

20 __ __ * _____

_____

_____

AUGUST 19

The last train ride I took was to . . .

20___ ___ * _____

_____

_____

_____

20___ ___ * _____

_____

_____

_____

20___ ___ * _____

_____

_____

_____

20___ ___ * _____

_____

_____

_____

20___ ___ * _____

_____

_____

_____

AUGUST 20

My favorite artist is . . .

20___ ___ * _____

_____

_____

20___ ___ * _____

_____

_____

20___ ___ * _____

_____

_____

20___ ___ * _____

_____

_____

20___ ___ * _____

_____

_____

I have a slight phobia about . . .

20___ ___ * _____

_____

_____

_____

20___ ___ * _____

_____

_____

_____

20___ ___ * _____

_____

_____

_____

20___ ___ * _____

_____

_____

_____

20___ ___ * _____

_____

_____

_____

AUGUST 22

The last photo I took was of . . . using my . . .

20___ ___ * _____

_____

_____

20___ ___ * _____

_____

_____

20___ ___ * _____

_____

_____

20___ ___ * _____

_____

_____

20___ ___ * _____

_____

_____

AUGUST 23

The last "touristy" place I visited was . . .

20___ ___ * _____

_____

_____

20___ ___ * _____

_____

_____

20___ ___ * _____

_____

_____

20___ ___ * _____

_____

_____

20___ ___ * _____

_____

_____

AUGUST 24

The most extreme weather I experienced recently was . . .

20___ ___ * _____

_____

_____

20___ ___ * _____

_____

_____

20___ ___ * _____

_____

_____

20___ ___ * _____

_____

_____

20___ ___ * _____

_____

_____

AUGUST 25

The last thing I downloaded was . . .

20__ __ * _____

_____

_____

_____

20__ __ * _____

_____

_____

_____

20__ __ * _____

_____

_____

_____

20__ __ * _____

_____

_____

_____

20__ __ * _____

_____

_____

_____

AUGUST 26

My favorite politician is . . . , but my
least favorite politician is . . .

20___ ___ * _____

_____

_____

20___ ___ * _____

_____

_____

20___ ___ * _____

_____

_____

20___ ___ * _____

_____

_____

20___ ___ * _____

_____

_____

AUGUST 27

The most recent person to tell me a secret was . . . about . . .

20__ __ * _____

_____

_____

20__ __ * _____

_____

_____

20__ __ * _____

_____

_____

20__ __ * _____

_____

_____

20__ __ * _____

_____

_____

AUGUST 28

If I could own any artwork in the world to look
at every day, it would have to be . . .

20___ ___ * _____

_____

_____

20___ ___ * _____

_____

_____

20___ ___ * _____

_____

_____

20___ ___ * _____

_____

_____

20___ ___ * _____

_____

_____

AUGUST 29

Recently someone asked for my advice about . . .

20___ ___ * _____

_____

_____

20___ ___ * _____

_____

_____

20___ ___ * _____

_____

_____

20___ ___ * _____

_____

_____

20___ ___ * _____

_____

_____

AUGUST 30

My favorite commercial is . . .

20___ ___ * _____

_____

_____

20___ ___ * _____

_____

_____

20___ ___ * _____

_____

_____

20___ ___ * _____

_____

_____

20___ ___ * _____

_____

_____

AUGUST 31

The website I use most often is . . .

20___ ___ * _____

_____

_____

20___ ___ * _____

_____

_____

20___ ___ * _____

_____

_____

20___ ___ * _____

_____

_____

20___ ___ * _____

_____

_____

SEPTEMBER 1

The last time I got super dressed up
was for . . . and I wore . . .

20 __ __ * _____

_____

_____

20 __ __ * _____

_____

_____

20 __ __ * _____

_____

_____

20 __ __ * _____

_____

_____

_____

20 __ __ * _____

_____

_____

_____

SEPTEMBER 2

The last conversation I had
with a stranger was about . . .

20___ ___ * _____

_____

_____

20___ ___ * _____

_____

_____

20___ ___ * _____

_____

_____

20___ ___ * _____

_____

_____

20___ ___ * _____

_____

_____

SEPTEMBER 3

Lately, my personality is . . .

20___ ___ * _____

_____

_____

20___ ___ * _____

_____

_____

20___ ___ * _____

_____

_____

20___ ___ * _____

_____

_____

20___ ___ * _____

_____

_____

SEPTEMBER 4

The most recent swear word I used was . . .

20___ ___ * _____

_____

_____

20___ ___ * _____

_____

_____

20___ ___ * _____

_____

_____

20___ ___ * _____

_____

_____

20___ ___ * _____

_____

_____

SEPTEMBER 5

The last time I pampered myself was when I . . .

20___ ___ * _____

_____

_____

20___ ___ * _____

_____

_____

20___ ___ * _____

_____

_____

20___ ___ * _____

_____

_____

20___ ___ * _____

_____

_____

My goal for next year is to . . .

20__ __ * _____

_____

_____

|||||||||||||||||||||||||||||||||||||||||||||||||||||||||||||||||||||||||||||||||

20__ __ * _____

_____

_____

|||||||||||||||||||||||||||||||||||||||||||||||||||||||||||||||||||||||||||||||||

20__ __ * _____

_____

_____

|||||||||||||||||||||||||||||||||||||||||||||||||||||||||||||||||||||||||||||||||

20__ __ * _____

_____

_____

|||||||||||||||||||||||||||||||||||||||||||||||||||||||||||||||||||||||||||||||||

20__ __ * _____

_____

_____

|||||||||||||||||||||||||||||||||||||||||||||||||||||||||||||||||||||||||||||||||

SEPTEMBER 7

My goal for this week is to . . . . .

20___ ___ * _____

_____

_____

_____

20___ ___ * _____

_____

_____

_____

20___ ___ * _____

_____

_____

_____

20___ ___ * _____

_____

_____

_____

20___ ___ * _____

_____

_____

_____

SEPTEMBER 8

A recent goal I achieved was . . .

20_____ * _____

_____

_____

||||||||||||||||||||||||||||||||||||||||||||||||||||||||||||||||||||||||||||||||||||||||||||||||||||

20_____ * _____

_____

_____

||||||||||||||||||||||||||||||||||||||||||||||||||||||||||||||||||||||||||||||||||||||||||||||||||||

20_____ * _____

_____

_____

||||||||||||||||||||||||||||||||||||||||||||||||||||||||||||||||||||||||||||||||||||||||||||||||||||

20_____ * _____

_____

_____

||||||||||||||||||||||||||||||||||||||||||||||||||||||||||||||||||||||||||||||||||||||||||||||||||||

20_____ * _____

_____

_____

||||||||||||||||||||||||||||||||||||||||||||||||||||||||||||||||||||||||||||||||||||||||||||||||||||

SEPTEMBER 9

A new pet peeve of mine is . . .

20___ ___ * _____

_____

_____

_____

20___ ___ * _____

_____

_____

_____

20___ ___ * _____

_____

_____

_____

20___ ___ * _____

_____

_____

_____

20___ ___ * _____

_____

_____

_____

SEPTEMBER 10

The last public speech I made was . . .

20___ ___ * _____

_____

_____

_____

20___ ___ * _____

_____

_____

_____

20___ ___ * _____

_____

_____

_____

20___ ___ * _____

_____

_____

_____

20___ ___ * _____

_____

_____

_____

SEPTEMBER 11

If I could choose a different occupation,
it would be to work as a . . .

20 __ __ * _____

_____

_____

20 __ __ * _____

_____

_____

20 __ __ * _____

_____

_____

20 __ __ * _____

_____

_____

20 __ __ * _____

_____

_____

The highlight of last weekend was . . .

20___ ___ * _____

_____

_____

20___ ___ * _____

_____

_____

20___ ___ * _____

_____

_____

20___ ___ * _____

_____

_____

20___ ___ * _____

_____

_____

SEPTEMBER 13

My most recent celebrity sighting was . . .

20___ ___ * _____

_____

_____

_____

20___ ___ * _____

_____

_____

_____

20___ ___ * _____

_____

_____

_____

20___ ___ * _____

_____

_____

_____

20___ ___ * _____

_____

_____

_____

If I could collect anything, I would be a collector of . . .

20___ ___ * _____

_____

_____

20___ ___ * _____

_____

_____

20___ ___ * _____

_____

_____

20___ ___ * _____

_____

_____

20___ ___ * _____

_____

_____

SEPTEMBER 15

I recently misplaced my . . .

20__ __ * _____

20__ __ * _____

20__ __ * _____

20__ __ * _____

20__ __ * _____

SEPTEMBER 16

I was right when I followed my intuition about . . .

20___ ___ * _____

_____

_____

_____

20___ ___ * _____

_____

_____

_____

20___ ___ * _____

_____

_____

_____

20___ ___ * _____

_____

_____

_____

20___ ___ * _____

_____

_____

_____

SEPTEMBER 17

The last time I stood up to someone it was . . . about . . .

20___ ___ * _____

_____

_____

20___ ___ * _____

_____

_____

20___ ___ * _____

_____

_____

20___ ___ * _____

_____

_____

20___ ___ * _____

_____

_____

SEPTEMBER 18

The last person I spoke to on the phone was . . .

20___ ___ * _____

_____

_____

|||||||||||||||||||||||||||||||||||||||||||||||||||||||||||||||||||||||||||||||||||||||||||||||||||

20___ ___ * _____

_____

_____

|||||||||||||||||||||||||||||||||||||||||||||||||||||||||||||||||||||||||||||||||||||||||||||||||||

20___ ___ * _____

_____

_____

|||||||||||||||||||||||||||||||||||||||||||||||||||||||||||||||||||||||||||||||||||||||||||||||||||

20___ ___ * _____

_____

_____

|||||||||||||||||||||||||||||||||||||||||||||||||||||||||||||||||||||||||||||||||||||||||||||||||||

20___ ___ * _____

_____

_____

|||||||||||||||||||||||||||||||||||||||||||||||||||||||||||||||||||||||||||||||||||||||||||||||||||

. . . is my good luck charm.

20 __ __ * _____

_____

_____

||||||||||||||||||||||||||||||||||||||||||||||||||||||||||||||||||||||||||||

20 __ __ * _____

_____

_____

||||||||||||||||||||||||||||||||||||||||||||||||||||||||||||||||||||||||||||

20 __ __ * _____

_____

_____

||||||||||||||||||||||||||||||||||||||||||||||||||||||||||||||||||||||||||||

20 __ __ * _____

_____

_____

||||||||||||||||||||||||||||||||||||||||||||||||||||||||||||||||||||||||||||

20 __ __ * _____

_____

_____

||||||||||||||||||||||||||||||||||||||||||||||||||||||||||||||||||||||||||||

SEPTEMBER 20

The last person I flirted with was . . .

20__ __ * _____

_____

_____

20__ __ * _____

_____

_____

20__ __ * _____

_____

_____

20__ __ * _____

_____

_____

20__ __ * _____

_____

_____

SEPTEMBER 21

The last time I went to the doctor was for . . .

20___ ___ * _____

_____

_____

_____

20___ ___ * _____

_____

_____

_____

20___ ___ * _____

_____

_____

_____

20___ ___ * _____

_____

_____

_____

20___ ___ * _____

_____

_____

_____

SEPTEMBER 22

My favorite scent is . . .

20___ ___ * _____

_____

_____

|||||||||||||||||||||||||||||||||||||||||||||||||||||||||||||||||||||||||||||||||

20___ ___ * _____

_____

_____

|||||||||||||||||||||||||||||||||||||||||||||||||||||||||||||||||||||||||||||||||

20___ ___ * _____

_____

_____

|||||||||||||||||||||||||||||||||||||||||||||||||||||||||||||||||||||||||||||||||

20___ ___ * _____

_____

_____

|||||||||||||||||||||||||||||||||||||||||||||||||||||||||||||||||||||||||||||||||

20___ ___ * _____

_____

_____

|||||||||||||||||||||||||||||||||||||||||||||||||||||||||||||||||||||||||||||||||

SEPTEMBER 23

. . . always seems to pop up in my dreams.

20___ ___ * _____

_____

_____

_____

20___ ___ * _____

_____

_____

_____

20___ ___ * _____

_____

_____

_____

20___ ___ * _____

_____

_____

_____

20___ ___ * _____

_____

_____

_____

SEPTEMBER 24

I typically wake up at . . . . . when . . . wakes me.

20 __ __ * _____

_____

_____

20 __ __ * _____

_____

_____

20 __ __ * _____

_____

_____

20 __ __ * _____

_____

_____

20 __ __ * _____

_____

_____

SEPTEMBER 25

This year I spent my birthday with . . .

20 __ __ * _____

_____

_____

20 __ __ * _____

_____

_____

20 __ __ * _____

_____

_____

20 __ __ * _____

_____

_____

20 __ __ * _____

_____

_____

SEPTEMBER 26

. . . recently brought tears to my eyes.

20__ __ * _____

_____

_____

_____

20__ __ * _____

_____

_____

_____

20__ __ * _____

_____

_____

_____

20__ __ * _____

_____

_____

_____

20__ __ * _____

_____

_____

_____

SEPTEMBER 27

The last visitor who came to my home was . . .

20 __ __ * _____

_____

_____

20 __ __ * _____

_____

_____

20 __ __ * _____

_____

_____

20 __ __ * _____

_____

_____

20 __ __ * _____

_____

_____

SEPTEMBER 28

The last person(s) I went out to dinner with was . . .

20___ ___ * _____
_____
_____
_____

20___ ___ * _____
_____
_____
_____

20___ ___ * _____
_____
_____
_____

20___ ___ * _____
_____
_____
_____

20___ ___ * _____
_____
_____
_____

SEPTEMBER 29

The nicest greeting card I received recently was from . . .

20__ __ * _____

_____

_____

20__ __ * _____

_____

_____

20__ __ * _____

_____

_____

20__ __ * _____

_____

_____

20__ __ * _____

_____

_____

The last time I blushed was when . . .

20___ ___ * _____

_____

_____

_____

20___ ___ * _____

_____

_____

_____

20___ ___ * _____

_____

_____

_____

20___ ___ * _____

_____

_____

_____

20___ ___ * _____

_____

_____

_____

OCTOBER 1

I get most of my news from . . .

20___ ___ * _____

_____

_____

_____

20___ ___ * _____

_____

_____

_____

20___ ___ * _____

_____

_____

_____

20___ ___ * _____

_____

_____

_____

20___ ___ * _____

_____

_____

_____

OCTOBER 2

I really felt physically drained recently after . . .

20___ ___ * _____

_____

_____

|||||||||||||||||||||||||||||||||||||||||||||||||||||||||||||||||||||||||||||||||||||||||||||||

20___ ___ * _____

_____

_____

|||||||||||||||||||||||||||||||||||||||||||||||||||||||||||||||||||||||||||||||||||||||||||||||

20___ ___ * _____

_____

_____

|||||||||||||||||||||||||||||||||||||||||||||||||||||||||||||||||||||||||||||||||||||||||||||||

20___ ___ * _____

_____

_____

|||||||||||||||||||||||||||||||||||||||||||||||||||||||||||||||||||||||||||||||||||||||||||||||

20___ ___ * _____

_____

_____

|||||||||||||||||||||||||||||||||||||||||||||||||||||||||||||||||||||||||||||||||||||||||||||||

OCTOBER 3

. . . totally amazes me.

20___ ___ * _____

_____

_____

20___ ___ * _____

_____

_____

20___ ___ * _____

_____

_____

20___ ___ * _____

_____

_____

20___ ___ * _____

_____

_____

OCTOBER 4

I am not sure I can forgive . . .

20____ ___ * _____
_____
_____

20____ ___ * _____
_____
_____

20____ ___ * _____
_____
_____

20____ ___ * _____
_____
_____

20____ ___ * _____
_____
_____

OCTOBER 5

After getting to know . . . better,
my opinion of them changed to . . .

20___ ___ * _____

_____

_____

20___ ___ * _____

_____

_____

20___ ___ * _____

_____

_____

20___ ___ * _____

_____

_____

20___ ___ * _____

_____

_____

OCTOBER 6

I would go to the ends of the earth for . . .

20___ ___ * _____

_____

_____

_____

20___ ___ * _____

_____

_____

_____

20___ ___ * _____

_____

_____

_____

20___ ___ * _____

_____

_____

_____

20___ ___ * _____

_____

_____

_____

OCTOBER 7

I really trust . . .

20 __ __ * _____

_____

_____

_____

20 __ __ * _____

_____

_____

_____

20 __ __ * _____

_____

_____

_____

20 __ __ * _____

_____

_____

_____

20 __ __ * _____

_____

_____

_____

OCTOBER 8

I am very skeptical about . . .

20___ ___ * _____

_____

_____

20___ ___ * _____

_____

_____

20___ ___ * _____

_____

_____

20___ ___ * _____

_____

_____

20___ ___ * _____

_____

_____

OCTOBER 9

Today I was intrigued by . . .

20___ ___ * _____

_____

_____

20___ ___ * _____

_____

_____

20___ ___ * _____

_____

_____

20___ ___ * _____

_____

_____

20___ ___ * _____

_____

_____

OCTOBER 10

When I am alone, I like to . . .

20___ ___ * _____

_____

_____

_____

20___ ___ * _____

_____

_____

_____

20___ ___ * _____

_____

_____

_____

20___ ___ * _____

_____

_____

_____

20___ ___ * _____

_____

_____

_____

OCTOBER 11

*If I could change genders for
a day, it would be fun to . . .*

20___ ___ * _____

_____

_____

_____

20___ ___ * _____

_____

_____

_____

20___ ___ * _____

_____

_____

_____

20___ ___ * _____

_____

_____

_____

20___ ___ * _____

_____

_____

_____

OCTOBER 12

My favorite clothing designer is . . .

20___ ___ * _____

_____

_____

_____

20___ ___ * _____

_____

_____

_____

20___ ___ * _____

_____

_____

_____

20___ ___ * _____

_____

_____

_____

20___ ___ * _____

_____

_____

_____

OCTOBER 13

*When I got home after being out most
recently, the first thing I did was . . .*

20 __ __ ＊ _____

_____

_____

_____

20 __ __ ＊ _____

_____

_____

_____

20 __ __ ＊ _____

_____

_____

_____

20 __ __ ＊ _____

_____

_____

_____

20 __ __ ＊ _____

_____

_____

_____

OCTOBER 14

The most exotic place I have been to is . . .

20___ ___ * _____

_____

_____

_____

20___ ___ * _____

_____

_____

_____

20___ ___ * _____

_____

_____

_____

20___ ___ * _____

_____

_____

_____

20___ ___ * _____

_____

_____

_____

A perfect lazy day is when I . . .

20 __ __ * _____

_____

_____

20 __ __ * _____

_____

_____

20 __ __ * _____

_____

_____

20 __ __ * _____

_____

_____

20 __ __ * _____

_____

_____

OCTOBER 16

. . . gives me butterflies.

20___ ___ * _____

_____

_____

_____

20___ ___ * _____

_____

_____

_____

20___ ___ * _____

_____

_____

_____

20___ ___ * _____

_____

_____

_____

20___ ___ * _____

_____

_____

_____

OCTOBER 17

I am envious of people who . . .

20 __ __ ＊ _____

_____

_____

20 __ __ ＊ _____

_____

_____

20 __ __ ＊ _____

_____

_____

20 __ __ ＊ _____

_____

_____

20 __ __ ＊ _____

_____

_____

OCTOBER 18

I recently felt a little shy in front of . . .

20__ __ * _____

_____

_____

20__ __ * _____

_____

_____

20__ __ * _____

_____

_____

20__ __ * _____

_____

_____

20__ __ * _____

_____

_____

OCTOBER 19

The last time I felt like a leader was when . . .

20___ ___ * _____

_____

_____

20___ ___ * _____

_____

_____

20___ ___ * _____

_____

_____

20___ ___ * _____

_____

_____

20___ ___ * _____

_____

_____

OCTOBER 20

The person who most recently said
"I love you" to me was . . .

20 __ __ * _____

_____

_____

_____

20 __ __ * _____

_____

_____

_____

20 __ __ * _____

_____

_____

_____

20 __ __ * _____

_____

_____

_____

20 __ __ * _____

_____

_____

_____

OCTOBER 21

The last time I had a big belly laugh was when . . .

20___ ___ * _____

_____

_____

_____

20___ ___ * _____

_____

_____

_____

20___ ___ * _____

_____

_____

_____

20___ ___ * _____

_____

_____

_____

20___ ___ * _____

_____

_____

_____

OCTOBER 22

One hour ago I was . . .

20__ __ * _____

_____

_____

20__ __ * _____

_____

_____

20__ __ * _____

_____

_____

20__ __ * _____

_____

_____

20__ __ * _____

_____

_____

The last person I hugged was . . .

20___ ___ * _____

_____

_____

20___ ___ * _____

_____

_____

20___ ___ * _____

_____

_____

20___ ___ * _____

_____

_____

20___ ___ * _____

_____

_____

OCTOBER 24

If I had a tag sale, the first thing I would get rid of is . . .

20___ ___ * _____

_____

_____

20___ ___ * _____

_____

_____

20___ ___ * _____

_____

_____

20___ ___ * _____

_____

_____

20___ ___ * _____

_____

_____

OCTOBER 25

I am tired of putting . . . on hold.

20 __ __ * _____

_____

_____

||||||||||||||||||||||||||||||||||||||||||||||||||||||||||||||||||||||||||||||||||||||||||||

20 __ __ * _____

_____

_____

||||||||||||||||||||||||||||||||||||||||||||||||||||||||||||||||||||||||||||||||||||||||||||

20 __ __ * _____

_____

_____

||||||||||||||||||||||||||||||||||||||||||||||||||||||||||||||||||||||||||||||||||||||||||||

20 __ __ * _____

_____

_____

||||||||||||||||||||||||||||||||||||||||||||||||||||||||||||||||||||||||||||||||||||||||||||

20 __ __ * _____

_____

_____

||||||||||||||||||||||||||||||||||||||||||||||||||||||||||||||||||||||||||||||||||||||||||||

This year work or school was . . .

20 ___ ___ * _____

_____

_____

20 ___ ___ * _____

_____

_____

20 ___ ___ * _____

_____

_____

20 ___ ___ * _____

_____

_____

20 ___ ___ * _____

_____

_____

OCTOBER 27

I feel like I always take care of . . .

20 __ __ * _____

_____

_____

20 __ __ * _____

_____

_____

20 __ __ * _____

_____

_____

20 __ __ * _____

_____

_____

20 __ __ * _____

_____

_____

OCTOBER 28

I deny myself . . . because . . .

20___ ___ * _____

_____

_____

_____

20___ ___ * _____

_____

_____

_____

20___ ___ * _____

_____

_____

_____

20___ ___ * _____

_____

_____

_____

20___ ___ * _____

_____

_____

_____

OCTOBER 29

I feel totally in control of . . .

20___ ___ * _____

_____

_____

20___ ___ * _____

_____

_____

20___ ___ * _____

_____

_____

20___ ___ * _____

_____

_____

20___ ___ * _____

_____

_____

OCTOBER 30

The most uncharacteristic thing I recently did was . . .

20___ ___ * _____

_____

_____

_____

20___ ___ * _____

_____

_____

_____

20___ ___ * _____

_____

_____

_____

20___ ___ * _____

_____

_____

_____

20___ ___ * _____

_____

_____

_____

OCTOBER 31

The spookiest thing that happened to me this year was . . .

20 __ __ * _____

_____

_____

20 __ __ * _____

_____

_____

20 __ __ * _____

_____

_____

20 __ __ * _____

_____

_____

20 __ __ * _____

_____

_____

NOVEMBER 1

. . . bores me to tears.

20___ ___ * _____

_____

_____

_____

20___ ___ * _____

_____

_____

_____

20___ ___ * _____

_____

_____

_____

20___ ___ * _____

_____

_____

_____

20___ ___ * _____

_____

_____

_____

I recently apologized to . . . for . . . ,
or . . . apologized to me.

20___ ___ * _____

_____

_____

20___ ___ * _____

_____

_____

20___ ___ * _____

_____

_____

20___ ___ * _____

_____

_____

20___ ___ * _____

_____

_____

NOVEMBER 3

The celebrity gossip headline of the day is . . .

20 __ __ * _____

_____

_____

20 __ __ * _____

_____

_____

20 __ __ * _____

_____

_____

20 __ __ * _____

_____

_____

20 __ __ * _____

_____

_____

NOVEMBER 4

The weirdest story I heard recently was . . .

20____ ____ * _____

_____

_____

20____ ____ * _____

_____

_____

20____ ____ * _____

_____

_____

20____ ____ * _____

_____

_____

20____ ____ * _____

_____

_____

NOVEMBER 5

I am probably too dependent on . . .

20___ ___ * _____

_____

_____

20___ ___ * _____

_____

_____

20___ ___ * _____

_____

_____

20___ ___ * _____

_____

_____

20___ ___ * _____

_____

_____

NOVEMBER 6

If I had a magic crystal ball, I would want to know . . .

20 __ __ * _____

_____

_____

_____

20 __ __ * _____

_____

_____

_____

20 __ __ * _____

_____

_____

_____

20 __ __ * _____

_____

_____

_____

20 __ __ * _____

_____

_____

_____

NOVEMBER 7

I never leave home without checking . . .

20 __ __ * _____

_____

_____

_____

20 __ __ * _____

_____

_____

_____

20 __ __ * _____

_____

_____

_____

20 __ __ * _____

_____

_____

_____

20 __ __ * _____

_____

_____

_____

NOVEMBER 8

The last game I played was . . .

20 __ __ * _____

_____

_____

_____

20 __ __ * _____

_____

_____

_____

20 __ __ * _____

_____

_____

_____

20 __ __ * _____

_____

_____

_____

20 __ __ * _____

_____

_____

_____

NOVEMBER 9

I recently gave myself . . . as a reward.

20___ ___ * _____

_____

_____

_____

20___ ___ * _____

_____

_____

_____

20___ ___ * _____

_____

_____

_____

20___ ___ * _____

_____

_____

_____

20___ ___ * _____

_____

_____

_____

NOVEMBER 10

The oddest thing in my home
that I cannot part with is . . .

20 __ __ * _____

_____

_____

_____

20 __ __ * _____

_____

_____

_____

20 __ __ * _____

_____

_____

_____

20 __ __ * _____

_____

_____

_____

20 __ __ * _____

_____

_____

_____

NOVEMBER 11

It would be cool to be . . . for a day.

20___ ___ * _____

_____

_____

_____

20___ ___ * _____

_____

_____

_____

20___ ___ * _____

_____

_____

_____

20___ ___ * _____

_____

_____

_____

20___ ___ * _____

_____

_____

_____

NOVEMBER 12

The last time I got lost was on the way to . . .

20___ ___ * _____

_____

_____

_____

20___ ___ * _____

_____

_____

_____

20___ ___ * _____

_____

_____

_____

20___ ___ * _____

_____

_____

_____

20___ ___ * _____

_____

_____

_____

NOVEMBER 13

If I owned a store, it would sell . . .

20＿ ＿ * _____

_____

_____

_____

20＿ ＿ * _____

_____

_____

_____

20＿ ＿ * _____

_____

_____

_____

20＿ ＿ * _____

_____

_____

_____

20＿ ＿ * _____

_____

_____

_____

NOVEMBER 14

*If I could give a gift to someone and money
was no object, I would give . . . a . . .*

20 ___ ___ * _____

_____

_____

20 ___ ___ * _____

_____

_____

20 ___ ___ * _____

_____

_____

20 ___ ___ * _____

_____

_____

20 ___ ___ * _____

_____

_____

NOVEMBER 15

My favorite traveling companion is . . .

20__ __ * _____

_____

_____

_____

20__ __ * _____

_____

_____

_____

20__ __ * _____

_____

_____

_____

20__ __ * _____

_____

_____

_____

20__ __ * _____

_____

_____

_____

NOVEMBER 16

The rudest thing someone did to me recently was . . .

20__ __ * _____

_____

_____

20__ __ * _____

_____

_____

20__ __ * _____

_____

_____

20__ __ * _____

_____

_____

20__ __ * _____

_____

_____

NOVEMBER 17

The most generous person I know is . . . because . . .

20 __ __ * _____

_____

_____

_____

20 __ __ * _____

_____

_____

_____

20 __ __ * _____

_____

_____

_____

20 __ __ * _____

_____

_____

_____

20 __ __ * _____

_____

_____

_____

NOVEMBER 18

I secretly harbor a desire for revenge against . . .

20___ ___ * _____

_____

_____

20___ ___ * _____

_____

_____

20___ ___ * _____

_____

_____

20___ ___ * _____

_____

_____

20___ ___ * _____

_____

_____

NOVEMBER 19

My most treasured photograph is of . . .

20 __ __ * _____

_____

_____

20 __ __ * _____

_____

_____

20 __ __ * _____

_____

_____

20 __ __ * _____

_____

_____

20 __ __ * _____

_____

_____

NOVEMBER 20

I recently volunteered to . . .

20___ ___ * _____

_____

_____

_____

20___ ___ * _____

_____

_____

_____

20___ ___ * _____

_____

_____

_____

20___ ___ * _____

_____

_____

_____

20___ ___ * _____

_____

_____

_____

If I had a chance, I would do . . . over again.

20＿＿ ＊ _____

_____

_____

_____

20＿＿ ＊ _____

_____

_____

_____

20＿＿ ＊ _____

_____

_____

_____

20＿＿ ＊ _____

_____

_____

_____

20＿＿ ＊ _____

_____

_____

_____

NOVEMBER 22

I would like to thank . . . for . . .

20 __ __ ＊ _____

_____

_____

_____

20 __ __ ＊ _____

_____

_____

_____

20 __ __ ＊ _____

_____

_____

_____

20 __ __ ＊ _____

_____

_____

_____

20 __ __ ＊ _____

_____

_____

_____

NOVEMBER 23

The last place I newly discovered—whether a street,
a shop, or a geographical location—was . . .

20___ ___ * _____

_____

_____

20___ ___ * _____

_____

_____

20___ ___ * _____

_____

_____

20___ ___ * _____

_____

_____

20___ ___ * _____

_____

_____

NOVEMBER 24

I would never want to own a . . .

20__ __ * _____

_____

_____

20__ __ * _____

_____

_____

20__ __ * _____

_____

_____

20__ __ * _____

_____

_____

20__ __ * _____

_____

_____

NOVEMBER 25

The first words I heard today were . . . spoken by . . .

20__ __ * _____

_____

_____

20__ __ * _____

_____

_____

20__ __ * _____

_____

_____

20__ __ * _____

_____

_____

20__ __ * _____

_____

_____

NOVEMBER 26

My favorite dessert lately is . . .

20___ ___ * _____

_____

_____

20___ ___ * _____

_____

_____

20___ ___ * _____

_____

_____

20___ ___ * _____

_____

_____

20___ ___ * _____

_____

_____

NOVEMBER 27

I spent my most recent evening
out with . . . and we went . . .

20___ ___ * _____

_____

_____

20___ ___ * _____

_____

_____

20___ ___ * _____

_____

_____

20___ ___ * _____

_____

_____

20___ ___ * _____

_____

_____

NOVEMBER 28

The top three things on my bucket list right now are . . .

20___ ___ * _____

_____

_____

20___ ___ * _____

_____

_____

20___ ___ * _____

_____

_____

20___ ___ * _____

_____

_____

20___ ___ * _____

_____

_____

NOVEMBER 29

The last interaction I had with a neighbor
was with . . . and we . . .

20___ ___ * _____

_____

_____

_____

20___ ___ * _____

_____

_____

_____

20___ ___ * _____

_____

_____

_____

20___ ___ * _____

_____

_____

_____

20___ ___ * _____

_____

_____

_____

If I could teach anything, I would love to teach . . . to . . .

20 __ __ * _____

_____

_____

_____

20 __ __ * _____

_____

_____

_____

20 __ __ * _____

_____

_____

_____

20 __ __ * _____

_____

_____

_____

20 __ __ * _____

_____

_____

_____

DECEMBER 1

I felt like a little bit of a rebel when I . . .

20___ ___ * _____

_____

_____

_____

20___ ___ * _____

_____

_____

_____

20___ ___ * _____

_____

_____

_____

20___ ___ * _____

_____

_____

_____

20___ ___ * _____

_____

_____

_____

DECEMBER 2

I am very optimistic about . . .

20 __ __ * _____

_____

_____

_____

20 __ __ * _____

_____

_____

_____

20 __ __ * _____

_____

_____

_____

20 __ __ * _____

_____

_____

_____

20 __ __ * _____

_____

_____

_____

DECEMBER 3

I recently questioned my belief in . . .

20____ ____ * _____

_____

_____

_____

20____ ____ * _____

_____

_____

_____

20____ ____ * _____

_____

_____

_____

20____ ____ * _____

_____

_____

_____

20____ ____ * _____

_____

_____

_____

DECEMBER 4

. . . is a new acquaintance of mine.

20__ __ * _____

_____

_____

_____

20__ __ * _____

_____

_____

_____

20__ __ * _____

_____

_____

_____

20__ __ * _____

_____

_____

_____

20__ __ * _____

_____

_____

_____

DECEMBER 5

A white lie I told recently was . . . to . . .

20__ __ * _____

_____

_____

_____

20__ __ * _____

_____

_____

_____

20__ __ * _____

_____

_____

_____

20__ __ * _____

_____

_____

_____

20__ __ * _____

_____

_____

_____

DECEMBER 6

The last time I asked for assistance, I asked . . . to . . .

20___ ___ * _____

_____

_____

20___ ___ * _____

_____

_____

20___ ___ * _____

_____

_____

20___ ___ * _____

_____

_____

20___ ___ * _____

_____

_____

DECEMBER 7

A close call I recently had was when . . .

20__ __ * _____
_____
_____

20__ __ * _____
_____
_____

20__ __ * _____
_____
_____

20__ __ * _____
_____
_____

20__ __ * _____
_____
_____

DECEMBER 8

If I was mayor of my town
the first thing I would do is . . .

20 __ __ * _____

_____

_____

20 __ __ * _____

_____

_____

20 __ __ * _____

_____

_____

20 __ __ * _____

_____

_____

20 __ __ * _____

_____

_____

DECEMBER 9

The last sports event I attended was . . .

20___ ___ * _____

_____

_____

_____

20___ ___ * _____

_____

_____

_____

20___ ___ * _____

_____

_____

_____

20___ ___ * _____

_____

_____

_____

20___ ___ * _____

_____

_____

_____

DECEMBER 10

I will give myself permission to . . .

20___ ___ * _____

_____

_____

20___ ___ * _____

_____

_____

20___ ___ * _____

_____

_____

20___ ___ * _____

_____

_____

20___ ___ * _____

_____

_____

DECEMBER 11

Right now I would rather be . . .

20___ ___ * _____

_____

_____

_____

20___ ___ * _____

_____

_____

_____

20___ ___ * _____

_____

_____

_____

20___ ___ * _____

_____

_____

_____

20___ ___ * _____

_____

_____

_____

DECEMBER 12

An inside joke I share with someone is . . . with . . .

20___ ___ * _____

_____

_____

_____

20___ ___ * _____

_____

_____

_____

20___ ___ * _____

_____

_____

_____

20___ ___ * _____

_____

_____

_____

20___ ___ * _____

_____

_____

_____

DECEMBER 13

*If the imaginary, fictional place of . . .
was real, I would like to visit.*

20__ __ * _____

_____

_____

20__ __ * _____

_____

_____

20__ __ * _____

_____

_____

20__ __ * _____

_____

_____

20__ __ * _____

_____

_____

DECEMBER 14

Recently, when I get bored I . . .

20___ ___ * _____

_____

_____

_____

20___ ___ * _____

_____

_____

_____

20___ ___ * _____

_____

_____

_____

20___ ___ * _____

_____

_____

_____

20___ ___ * _____

_____

_____

_____

DECEMBER 15

I was happiest this week when . . .

20___ ___ * _____

_____

_____

_____

20___ ___ * _____

_____

_____

_____

20___ ___ * _____

_____

_____

_____

20___ ___ * _____

_____

_____

_____

20___ ___ * _____

_____

_____

_____

DECEMBER 16

I recently made a promise to . . . to . . .

20___ ___ * _____

_____

_____

20___ ___ * _____

_____

_____

20___ ___ * _____

_____

_____

20___ ___ * _____

_____

_____

20___ ___ * _____

_____

_____

DECEMBER 17

Something healthy I did for myself this week was . . .

20___ ___ ✳ _____

_____

_____

20___ ___ ✳ _____

_____

_____

20___ ___ ✳ _____

_____

_____

20___ ___ ✳ _____

_____

_____

20___ ___ ✳ _____

_____

_____

DECEMBER 18

... was my favorite month this year because ...

20 __ __ * _____

_____

_____

_____

20 __ __ * _____

_____

_____

_____

20 __ __ * _____

_____

_____

_____

20 __ __ * _____

_____

_____

_____

20 __ __ * _____

_____

_____

_____

DECEMBER 19

I need to recommit to . . .

20___ ___ * _____

_____

_____

20___ ___ * _____

_____

_____

20___ ___ * _____

_____

_____

20___ ___ * _____

_____

_____

20___ ___ * _____

_____

_____

DECEMBER 20

An excuse I gave someone recently was . . .

20___ ___ * _____

_____

_____

20___ ___ * _____

_____

_____

20___ ___ * _____

_____

_____

20___ ___ * _____

_____

_____

20___ ___ * _____

_____

_____

DECEMBER 21

If I could make someone do something,
I would make . . . do . . .

20___ ___ * _____

_____

_____

20___ ___ * _____

_____

_____

20___ ___ * _____

_____

_____

20___ ___ * _____

_____

_____

20___ ___ * _____

_____

_____

DECEMBER 22

I have been procrastinating about . . .

20___ ___ * _____

_____

_____

20___ ___ * _____

_____

_____

20___ ___ * _____

_____

_____

20___ ___ * _____

_____

_____

20___ ___ * _____

_____

_____

DECEMBER 23

I recently said yes to . . .

20___ ___ * _____

_____

_____

_____

20___ ___ * _____

_____

_____

_____

20___ ___ * _____

_____

_____

_____

20___ ___ * _____

_____

_____

_____

20___ ___ * _____

_____

_____

_____

DECEMBER 24

I recently said no to . . .

20___ ___ * _____

_____

_____

_____

20___ ___ * _____

_____

_____

_____

20___ ___ * _____

_____

_____

_____

20___ ___ * _____

_____

_____

_____

20___ ___ * _____

_____

_____

_____

DECEMBER 25

The last time I felt like I had
a guardian angel was when . . .

20 __ __ * _____

_____

_____

_____

20 __ __ * _____

_____

_____

_____

20 __ __ * _____

_____

_____

_____

20 __ __ * _____

_____

_____

_____

20 __ __ * _____

_____

_____

_____

DECEMBER 26

. . . gives me a serene feeling

20__ __ * _____
_____
_____
|||||||||||||||||||||||||||||||||||||||||||||||||||||||||||||||||||||||||||||||||||||||

20__ __ * _____
_____
_____
|||||||||||||||||||||||||||||||||||||||||||||||||||||||||||||||||||||||||||||||||||||||

20__ __ * _____
_____
_____
|||||||||||||||||||||||||||||||||||||||||||||||||||||||||||||||||||||||||||||||||||||||

20__ __ * _____
_____
_____
|||||||||||||||||||||||||||||||||||||||||||||||||||||||||||||||||||||||||||||||||||||||

20__ __ * _____
_____
_____
|||||||||||||||||||||||||||||||||||||||||||||||||||||||||||||||||||||||||||||||||||||||

DECEMBER 27

I would love to makeover...

20___ ___ ✳ _____

_____

_____

20___ ___ ✳ _____

_____

_____

20___ ___ ✳ _____

_____

_____

20___ ___ ✳ _____

_____

_____

20___ ___ ✳ _____

_____

_____

DECEMBER 28

I wish I could read . . .'s mind.

20___ ___ * _____

_____

_____

_____

20___ ___ * _____

_____

_____

_____

20___ ___ * _____

_____

_____

_____

20___ ___ * _____

_____

_____

_____

20___ ___ * _____

_____

_____

_____

DECEMBER 29

*The last time I copied what someone
did, I copied . . . and did . . .*

20___ ___ * _____

_____

_____

_____

20___ ___ * _____

_____

_____

_____

20___ ___ * _____

_____

_____

_____

20___ ___ * _____

_____

_____

_____

20___ ___ * _____

_____

_____

_____

DECEMBER 30

A story I told recently was about when . . . and I told . . .

20___ ___ * _____

_____

_____

|||||||||||||||||||||||||||||||||||||||||||||||||||||||||||||||||||||||||||||||||||||||

20___ ___ * _____

_____

_____

|||||||||||||||||||||||||||||||||||||||||||||||||||||||||||||||||||||||||||||||||||||||

20___ ___ * _____

_____

_____

|||||||||||||||||||||||||||||||||||||||||||||||||||||||||||||||||||||||||||||||||||||||

20___ ___ * _____

_____

_____

|||||||||||||||||||||||||||||||||||||||||||||||||||||||||||||||||||||||||||||||||||||||

20___ ___ * _____

_____

_____

|||||||||||||||||||||||||||||||||||||||||||||||||||||||||||||||||||||||||||||||||||||||

DECEMBER 31

Today I see the glass half- . . .

20___ ___ * _____

_____

_____

20___ ___ * _____

_____

_____

20___ ___ * _____

_____

_____

20___ ___ * _____

_____

_____

20___ ___ * _____

_____

_____